THE BEST FROM

GOOSEBERRY HILL

Patterns for Stuffed Animals & Dolls

By
Kathy Pace

C&T PUBLISHING

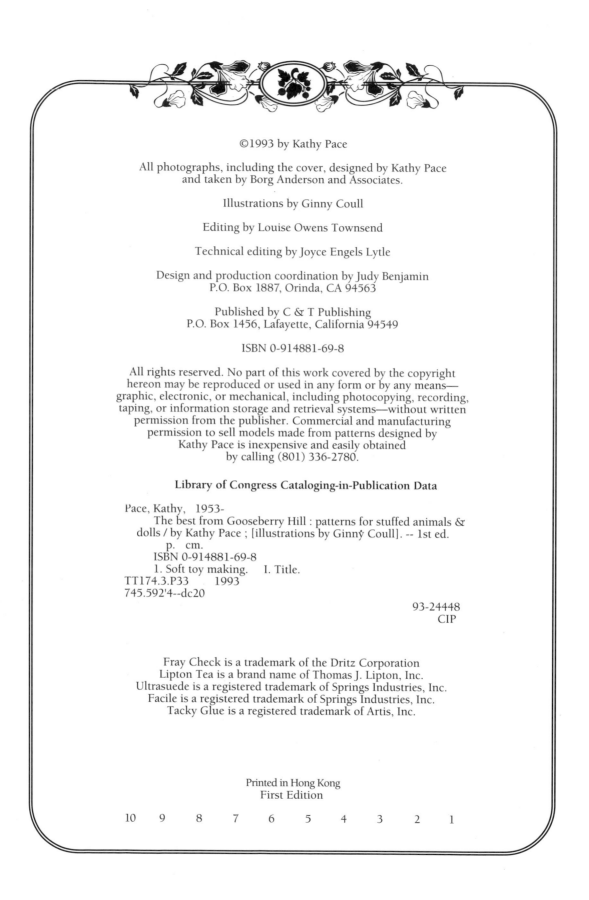

©1993 by Kathy Pace

All photographs, including the cover, designed by Kathy Pace
and taken by Borg Anderson and Associates.

Illustrations by Ginny Coull

Editing by Louise Owens Townsend

Technical editing by Joyce Engels Lytle

Design and production coordination by Judy Benjamin
P.O. Box 1887, Orinda, CA 94563

Published by C & T Publishing
P.O. Box 1456, Lafayette, California 94549

ISBN 0-914881-69-8

Library of Congress Cataloging-in-Publication Data

Pace, Kathy, 1953-
    The best from Gooseberry Hill : patterns for stuffed animals &
dolls / by Kathy Pace ; [illustrations by Ginny Coull]. -- 1st ed.
        p.   cm.
    ISBN 0-914881-69-8
    1. Soft toy making.   I. Title.
TT174.3.P33   1993
745.592'4--dc20

                                                                93-24448
                                                                CIP

Printed in Hong Kong
First Edition

10   9   8   7   6   5   4   3   2   1

TABLE OF CONTENTS

The Color Section begins on page 33.

This book is dedicated to

all of our friends and fans who

have purchased Gooseberry Hill

patterns over the last 12 years.

~

Thank you for encouraging

us to continue designing and

making our patterns available.

We couldn't do it without you.

I am grateful to Dennis for
leaving his life's work to help me
with my "little business" and for all
of his love and support!

Thanks to my daughter Tahna for her help
with the typing, which was a lifesaver.

Thanks to each of my boys for being independent
while Amber and I worked on the book.

My special thanks to my daughter Amber for helping me
write this book. She gave up many evenings and holidays to
see that the work progressed. I would never have attempted
this project without her help. I realize it was a real sacrifice
of her time during her senior year of high school.

I appreciate Amy's help with sewing the samples
and the typing. She is a dear friend.

I'm so happy that my mother taught me how to sew.
She demonstrated that joy comes through being creative,
and she taught me that I could do anything
I wanted to do if I would only try.

I thank my Heavenly Father for blessing me
with talent and this opportunity.

∽

Kathy Pace
Coalville, Utah
Spring 1993

INTRODUCTION:
$\mathscr{S}$AVORING THE PAST

The question customers ask me most often is, "Where do you get your ideas?" Each new design results from some specific object that charms me. Since childhood I have fantasized about living in "the olden days." I love the old things that were made to be beautiful as well as functional: long dresses and lace-up boots, wagon wheels, lanterns, handmade laces, shell buttons, and pieced quilts. My Grandma Shaw's pie safe with the mouse hole in the top drawer is more beautiful to me than a polished, brand-new chest could ever be.

When the railroad was completed to the West and the last golden spike was driven, the rails brought some of life's greatest luxuries to women who hungered for beautiful things — at least, to those who could afford them. They decorated their homes with Victorian tapestries, fringes, ferns, oval picture frames, ornate clocks, and intricately carved furniture. They began to wear stylish hats and leg-of-mutton sleeves, opera capes and ostrich fans, velvet evening bags, and Battenberg laces.

In designing patterns, I have held the love of the past in my thoughts. I can picture each item I create in a 19th-century home. Here in Utah, we are constantly aware of pioneer days, when the women had to make their children's clothes and toys from whatever was at hand. I love the homespun, tiny-print calicoes and rough osnaburg from that earlier era, fully as much as I love the beautiful luxuries of the post-railroad days.

Facing Page: The author treasures this photograph of three generations of the Shelton family because they are her ancestors. Standing from the left are her grandmother's sister, Nona; her great-great-grandmother, Elizabeth Rogers Smith; her grandmother, Oma Ellen Shelton Shaw; and her grandmother's brother, Will. Seated are her great-grandfather, Charles Lonzo Shelton, and her great-grandmother, Rebecca Elizabeth Smith Shelton.

Sometimes a special antique object inspires me with a pattern idea. I found an old muslin blouse in a flour sack with some cloth salt bags and flour sacks that were to be used for rags, and it became the model for my 1890s Blouse pattern. When my girls were babies, I wished for an antique christening gown pattern. One day I came across an old photograph of a cherubic trio of babies, all dressed in dainty white batiste dresses long enough to cover their mothers' knees modestly. I combined elements of a couple of the dresses with some imagination to complete our Christening Gown pattern.

As I introduce our most popular designs in this book, I'll also tell you how they came about. When we prepare a pattern for individual packet sales, we have to consider space restrictions; therefore, we can't give very many of our ideas for color combinations, trimming, embellishing, or displaying the completed projects. In this book we have room to convey to you some of these stimulating ideas. Many sewers, especially quilters, tell me that they never cut up their patterns. They like to keep everything on the original sheet so the little pieces don't get lost. This book will also serve, then, as a permanent collection of our very best work.

Gooseberry Hill Sewing Adventures
From Geese to Glass Buttons

During the winter of 1980, A close friend needed a centerpiece for a special Christmas dinner. She had seen some cloth geese in a gift shop, but she thought they were overpriced. Knowing that I could sew, she asked if I could make her a cloth goose. I had made only a few stuffed toys in my life, but I said I'd try. First, I called fabric shops in the area and asked if they had a pattern, but I found to my dismay that there were none. I gathered up my pencil and a sketch pad, and I walked down the lane by Silver Creek to the place where our neighbor's geese were nesting. I'm afraid I sketched the neck a little long, because they stretch their necks out to scare off intruders like me. (On the version in this book I shortened the neck considerably.)

The first attempt looked like a cross between a snail and a dinosaur. I made the body with a gusset, or center section, to make it sit without tipping. I left off the wings so it would look more regal if made out of moiré taffeta or velvet (although I did add wings to Little Goose, my second design).

With some corrections, the next one, made from a red fabric with white pindots, looked a lot more like a goose. Then came my favorite part, the trimmings. For the holidays I tied a red plaid bow around the goose's neck and tucked in baby's breath and long cinnamon sticks. I sometimes used silk flowers and a combination of ribbons to make the bow. Imagine that goose made out of milk-chocolate linen with a black beak and eyes, sporting a forest and cranberry plaid bow tied to a round brass hunting horn wrapped with decorator ivy.

After my friend's party, she asked for a few copies of the pattern for her guests, who loved the centerpiece. She said, "I'll bet you could sell a lot of these patterns in Salt Lake City." It was worth a try. Her husband, a talented artist, drew the cover goose and hand-printed the instructions. The first printing of the Country Goose cost $40. I had to borrow $20 from my husband because I had only $20 of babysitting money of my "own." After I hand-folded and delivered the first orders, I paid back that $20 loan and was so excited: I was in business!

No one could believe how those patterns "flew out of the shops." The Goose was a great success, and I felt encouraged to try other barnyard animals, since country decorating was just taking off. With that in mind, I created the geese, chickens, a cat, the stick pony, the cow and pony pull toys, and even a turkey. I called them my Farm Flock Collection. It was such a thrill to receive requests for information on my pattern line from all across the country. Many of the requests came from tourists who had seen some of the patterns while visiting Mormon Handicraft near Temple Square in Salt Lake City. When I realized how easy it was to ship to other states and how much people liked my patterns, I decided to advertise in trade magazines to attract the attention of more shops outside of Utah. During the

first year, 400 shops started to order from my small business. I soon had to change from hand-drawn black-and-white to full-color covers, so one of my first purchases was a good camera. The business name I was using at that time was a carryover from my California boutique days, Kathy's Crafts.

Eventually I realized that my name and covers needed to have a more professional look. When we built our home in a high valley of the Uinta Mountains, I decided to name both the home and the business Gooseberry Hill: Goose for the first successful pattern, and Berry because my husband wanted to cover the hill with strawberries. When we started, our children were very small, all five of them under 8 years old. Those were busy days! Sometimes the baby would be rocked to sleep on my knees under the sewing machine. I did the running from printer to shops, all the invoicing, mailing, sewing, designing, and advertising. I often had fabric and the sewing machine on the kitchen table when my husband came home from work, instead of his hoped-for dinner. Dennis really couldn't understand what in the world I thought I could achieve by "all of this." You can imagine how great I felt when I purchased my own used car.

It sure was nice to hear him ask if there was anything he could do to help me with my "little business"! Before long, he was able to come to work for me full-time. He now manages all aspects of the business except the sewing, and with his help, Gooseberry Hill has blossomed into a big business. We now ship to thousands of stores, with accounts in several foreign countries. I create a few designs each year for McCall's Pattern Company, and it has been exciting to see my mother and two of my sisters begin designing for them recently as well.

When we travel to international market shows, we always take a few days to browse in antique shops. Dennis and I add to our doll collection and gather quantities of old glass buttons, which I use on my new designs. We also hunt for handmade lace, old toys, and furnishings.

I realize that all of my success is due to the fact that someone is willing to purchase my patterns. I am always so surprised and pleased when discriminating sewers choose to make Gooseberry Hill patterns. I hope you will be pleased with the patterns in this book, and that I can create new projects that you will enjoy making, giving, and keeping.

BASIC SEWING INSTRUCTIONS

Always read through all of the instructions before beginning a project. Try other layouts in order to fit the paper pattern pieces on the recommended fabric yardage.

• **Seam Allowances**: All of the pattern pieces in this book, even those you draw yourself from dimensions given, have *1/4" seam allowances included.* We suggest that you measure the distance from your sewing-machine needle to the edge of the presser foot. Often this is 1/4". If it is not, you may see where the edge of the fabric should be in relationship to the presser foot, and you may wish to mark it with a piece of masking tape. Be accurate, as different seam allowances will change the size and look of the finished product.

• **Trimming and Clipping**: After sewing an item, you'll need to clip and trim the seams. Outside curves look best if they are trimmed off a little so that only 1/8" seam allowance remains. Inside curves need to be clipped: Snip toward the seam allowance every 1/4" to 1/2". Some sharp curves, such as those on a hand or glove pattern, need to be clipped three times very closely so you can turn right side out neatly.

• **Symbols**: Arrows indicate the straight grain of the fabric. Pattern pieces may be laid parallel to the selvage or at right angles to it.

When you see the word *fold* on top of two connecting arrows with the words "place on the fold" below, this pattern piece must be cut with this edge on a fold of fabric. Make sure that folds are also on the straight of grain. You may want to trace such pattern pieces onto a folded piece of paper; then, when you are cutting small pieces, the entire piece can be laid out flat instead of being placed on the fold. Check to see if you cut one or two pieces to save fabric.

• **Measured Patterns**: When measurements are given for a pattern instead of a pattern piece, they are usually for a simple rectangle for a skirt or slip. Remember that all necessary seam allowances have been included in the given measurements. Mark the piece with a ruler and cut using a rotary cutter from the end of the fabric yardage, starting from the fold to the selvages, before cutting the other little pieces.

• **Narrow Hem**: To make a narrow hem, you should turn the edge under twice 1/8" to 1/4" to the wrong side and sew it with a straight stitch. We generally use a narrow hemming foot, which takes much less time and a little less fabric, but I don't make any length adjustments. You are dealing with too little length to worry about.

• **Gathering**: Sew a long basting stitch in one layer of fabric where indicated to gather it. Backstitch at the end of the piece. Pull gently on the bobbin thread until the gathers (shearing) are even, and the first piece matches the length of the piece it is being sewn to.

• **Casings**: A casing is formed by turning down the top of a slip or pants 1/4" and pressing. Turn it down 1/2" and sew near the 1/4" fold to have a casing to run the elastic through.

• **Cutting**: I use a rotary cutter and cutting mat for 99% of my cutting: this speeds the process considerably. Small-diameter blades are easier to control with all of the small curves in my designs, but large-diameter blades will cut through many fabric thicknesses and through fur much more easily than the small ones.

• **Skin-Colored Fabric**: This shade can be obtained by putting five yards of muslin in the washer on a small-load cycle with hot water and one box of tan fabric dye. A smaller amount of fabric could be done in a bowl with a smaller ration of dye. I use this color for my Santas and elves.

• **Slits**: Some slits are indicated for ease in turning things right side out. Note where they are, and cut the slit through only the top layer of fabric.

• **Tools**: Hemostat forceps can be very useful in dollmaking. They look like tiny long-nosed pliers; they will reach into small places and lock onto the fabric so you can turn things inside out easily. Ask at your local quilt shop or fabric store for turning tools. The forceps are also available from a medical supply shop.

• **Stuffing**: The material used to stuff your dolls should be of high quality for a smooth, finished look. If you have lumps, there are usually three possible reasons: you have wadded the stuffing into a ball before placing it into the doll; you don't have enough stuffing in it; or your stuffing is of poor quality. Try to put the stuffing into your doll gently, but pack it in fairly tightly — not seam-bursting tight, but enough to create a plump, smooth figure. However, faces that will have to be sculpted should be filled loosely, and bear bodies, arms, and legs will have a more traditional look if you stuff them lightly to create a purposeful slouch and sag.

TAPESTRY GOOSE

©1993 Kathy Pace

This goose looks terrific in so many kinds of fabrics. It would be fun to make in charcoal gray, burgundy, or forest green cotton. Wrap ivy and grape-vines around the neck; wire on pomegranates, grapes, pears, and bundles of wheat or other grains tied up with raffia or a paper bow. Patterned corduroys in dark blacks or grays would make a beautiful goose, too. (More ideas for decorating the goose appear in the "Gooseberry Hill Sewing Adventures" section on pages 7 and 8.)

For a spring centerpiece, the goose looks beautiful in a light-colored tapestry print. Use a grapevine wreath as a nest, with ivy and ferns tucked between the vines. Artificial flowers and berries could be added to complement the colors in the fabric print.

SUPPLY LIST

1/8 yd. or scrap of fabric for beak

1/2 yd. tapestry fabric for body

Two 12mm safety eyes (optional)

1 1/2 lbs. stuffing

Matching thread

NOTE: Zigzag or serge around all outside edges of tapestry body pieces.

Cutting Instructions: All pattern pieces will be found on the pull-out pages at the back of this book. Cut two side bodies, and cut a slit in the neck as indicated. Cut two breast sections. Cut two beaks from contrasting fabric.

1a. Fold one neck right sides together on slit line and sew dart from A to B.

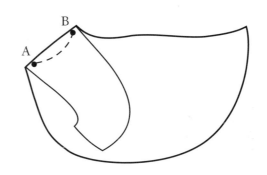

1b. Sew beak to head right sides together matching notch and dots L and M. Repeat for other side body.

2a. Sew two breast sections right sides together on notched edge from C to D.

C

D

2b. Pin one side of breast to one side body matching dots C and D. Sew, leaving an opening between dots E and F; backstitch at dots C and D. Clip seam allowance to dots C and D.

C

D

E F

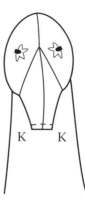

K K

3b. Fold beak flat, with dots G and J matching right sides together and raw edges of beak ends even. Sew from K to K backstitching at both ends. Turn the goose right side out, and stuff firmly. Try to keep the bottom flat. Whipstitch opening closed. You may twist the neck slightly (so the goose looks off to one side) by holding the head and body and twisting them in opposite directions.

3a. Pin remaining edge of breast to second side body, right sides together, matching dots C and D. Pin side bodies together from G on beak to D at tail, and from J on beak to C at breast. Sew from G all around body to J as shown. Clip seam allowances every 1/2" along curves. (*Optional:* Put safety eyes in at eye dots.) Clip seam allowances free at dots C and D.

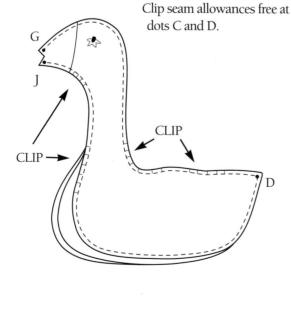

G

J

CLIP

CLIP

D

Running to the window, he opened it, and put
out his head. No fog, no mist; clear, bright, jovial,
stirring; cold, cold, piping for the blood to dance to;
golden sunlight, heavenly sky, sweet fresh air;
merry bells. Oh, glorious!

—Charles Dickens

~

Things that matter most must never be at the
mercy of things that matter least.

—Johann Wolfgang von Goethe

VIOLET BUNNY

©1989 Kathy Pace

Morning Glory, A Bunny To Love

Once, returning from a two-week combination vacation and business trip with our five young children and all of our trade-show booth supplies and samples crammed into our family van, we stopped at an antique shop called Grannie's in west Texas. The kids piled out of the van to stretch their legs while I browsed through Grannie's wonderful assortment of dishes, quilts, old furniture, and books. I found a darling child-sized wooden chair. It was unassuming and plain, the wood worn to a velvety smoothness by many little hands. As we loaded everyone back into the van, I realized that my antiquing stops might soon have to end — for this trip, that is. (I'll admit we had already stopped more than a few times; I can't seem to pass by an antique shop without stopping.) The problem was that there was simply not any room for my chair. Prior to this stop I had quickly arranged and re-arranged our overflowing cargo to make sure I had room for that "one more treasure," but we had really reached our limit. So, I uncomplainingly climbed in and rode with the chair on my lap. After all, we had only 700 miles to go.

With that chair on my lap, I began to think of what I could make to put on it. I immediately thought of an ornate child-sized rabbit, since I have always loved Beatrix Potter's delicate watercolor illustrations of Peter Rabbit and his family. I imagined a sweet, fat bunny, about the size of a 2-year-old, with long ears drooping down her back and big feet sticking out from under her pink cabbage-rose chintz dress. She would have a beautiful lace collar and pinafore of the Battenberg laces that were becoming so popular. I envisioned a dainty little babies' breath wreath on her head, since she was a meadow creature and would undoubtedly love daisy chains and curled ribbons. Shifting everything a bit to retrieve pencil and paper from my purse, I sketched her and

hoped that I could make her as delightful as she was in my imagination. As soon as my children went back to school that fall, I began working on my fantasy bunny, who later came to be known as Morning Glory, a Bunny to Love. She fits my imagined picture perfectly!

Victorian Baby Bunnies

For this book I chose to include the Victorian Baby Bunny, which evolved from the much larger Morning Glory pattern. A few people had called to say that, although they loved Morning Glory, their rooms were too small for a large bunny. A smaller version had to be born. One might think that all I had to do was make a trip to the copy center to reduce Morning Glory to a baby-sized rabbit; however, if you've ever tried something like that, you were probably as surprised as I was to find that the proportions didn't work at all as they got smaller. With some juggling, the little bunnies took shape. By far the most popular one is Violet, who is included in this book with her dress and petticoat. She has all the charm — and then some — of her mother Morning Glory.

My favorite dress for Violet is a dark lavender tiny print. The white lace ruffle and insert stand out in beautiful contrast to the dark dress and ribbon. But the most darling Violet we ever made was a milk-chocolate-colored one with a white dress. We put some narrow lace on the skirt hem and tied a lace bow around her head. For her feet and inside her paws and ears, we used a very pale peach cotton. In an antique shop I found a little gold locket with the initials BB, which I put on a little satin ribbon that I tied in a bow. This was pinned over our bunny's heart.

One sewing friend wrote to tell me how she used the bodice front and back patterns without the sleeve, and added a gathered tulle skirt for a ballerina costume. I've seen many photos of bunnies made from this pattern by seamstresses from all over the country. It is fun to see their creative touches and inventive accessories: canes, umbrellas, flowered hats, shoes, and handbags. Their bodies were make out of calico prints, tapestry, brushed nylon, or velvet. What's your inspiration?

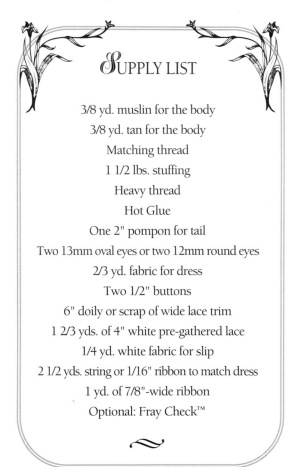

SUPPLY LIST

3/8 yd. muslin for the body

3/8 yd. tan for the body

Matching thread

1 1/2 lbs. stuffing

Heavy thread

Hot Glue

One 2" pompon for tail

Two 13mm oval eyes or two 12mm round eyes

2/3 yd. fabric for dress

Two 1/2" buttons

6" doily or scrap of wide lace trim

1 2/3 yds. of 4" white pre-gathered lace

1/4 yd. white fabric for slip

2 1/2 yds. string or 1/16" ribbon to match dress

1 yd. of 7/8"-wide ribbon

Optional: Fray Check™

Violet Bunny's Body Instructions

Cutting Instructions: Pattern pieces are on pages 20-24. Cut body parts as indicated on pattern pieces. You should have: two side heads, two muslin ears, two tan ears, one head underside, four legs, two feet, two muslin arms, two tan arms, one body and two side bodies.

1. Layer both tan ears on top of muslin ears making sure angles at bottom of ears are opposite. Sew around ear from A to B, trim off tip of ear near stitching. Turn right side out, press, repeat for other ear.

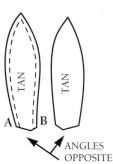

2. Mark eye dots in side head. Cut ear slit in side heads. Cut slit in head underside. Use Fray Check™ around edges. Fold ear on fold line toward muslin. Place folded ear on right side of one head with raw edge of ear extending 1/8" beyond slit. Edge of ear should just touch end of slit. Fold head over ear. With raw edges of slit even, sew ear dart. Backstitch at end of dart. Repeat with other ear and remaining side head. Put safety shank eyes in place now.

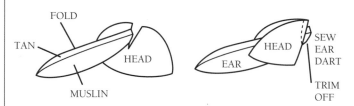

3a. Matching ear darts and placing right sides together, sew heads together from A over the top to B. Trim seam allowance, match and pin ear darts to match at top of head.

3b. Pin head underside to sideheads, matching A to A and B to B. Roll ears up and stuff inside head. Sew from A around head and back to A with underside flat on machine. Clip seam allowance free at nose. Turn right side out through slit in underside, stuff firmly. Whip opening closed. With a strong double thread or single crochet thread and a long craft needle, tie a knot and go into head near the slit on the underside. Do a backstitch, come out under the edge of the eye, go back in 1/8" away, and come out under the edge of the opposite eye. Go back down and out near the slit. Pull thread until eyes form slight indentations. Backstitch and tie knot.

4. Referring to drawing at top of facing page, come out near seam for nose at A, 5/8" up from underside seam and almost 3/8" out. Make a V-shaped stitch held at the bottom by a tiny stitch. Go in at B, out at C, in at D, and out under head near slit. Pull, and work stuffing into the nose

with the needle. Tie off by knotting firmly under head. Eyelashes and whiskers are made by taking one stitch with double quilting thread. Tie a knot 2" from end of thread. Take a stitch 1/2" long into head, come out, and tie another knot. Trim ends. Do this above eyes for eyelashes and in cheek area. Refer to color photo.

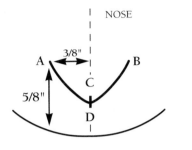

5a. Pin, then sew center section to one side body matching dots A and D.

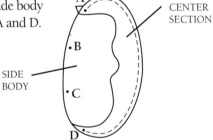

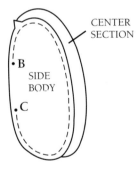

5b. Pin remaining side body to free edge of center section, matching notch and dots B and C on side bodies. Sew all around from B to C. Turn right side out and stuff firmly. Whipstitch opening closed. Set aside.

6a. Cut slits in two legs as indicated on pattern. Lay down plain legs with toes going the opposite way. Pin one leg with a slit on top of the plain leg. Sew from dot A on around top to B. Clip as shown.

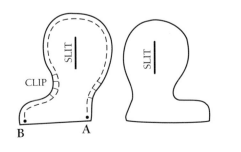

6b. Pin foot into opening, matching A to A and B to B. Sew. Make other leg the same as the first one. Turn right side out, stuff firmly, whipstitch opening closed.

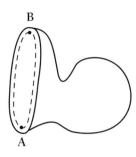

6c. Lay muslin arms out opposite each other. Place tan arm on top, of each muslin arm. Sew from A all around arm to B, leaving opening between A and B. Clip inside elbow, trim off seam allowance around paw end. Turn right side out. Stuff paw to line, sew across line, finish stuffing and whip opening closed. Repeat for other arm.

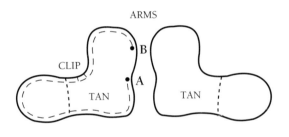

7. Glue arms to body 1" down from head on sides of body with muslin side of arm next to body. Glue pompon to body at back. Glue legs to body using a large circle of hot glue, having body and legs resting on table. Feet should extend approximately 3" beyond body. Hot glue head to top of body. The narrow end of the body goes up.

Violet Bunny's Dress

Cutting Instructions: Cut two bodice backs on fold, cut two sleeves on fold and two bodice fronts on fold. Cut one lace insert from doily or wide lace. No patterns are given for skirt or slip. Cut 8" x 45" rectangle for skirt. Cut 5" x 45" rectangle for slip.

1. With sleeve wrong side up, lay a 12" string or 1/16" ribbon across the hem. Fold hem over string 1/2". Sew near raw edge of fabric to form casing, being careful to not catch string in hem. Backstitch at beginning and end. Repeat for other sleeve. Machine baste upper curved edge of sleeve. Draw up bobbin thread to gather top edge. Repeat on other sleeve, set aside.

SLEEVE

2. Place lace insert on right side of one bodice front, neck edges even. Sew two back bodices to this front bodice at shoulder seams, right sides together.

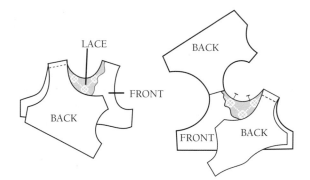

3. Cut two 6" lengths of gathered 4" lace. Trim off corners of bound edge of lace as shown.

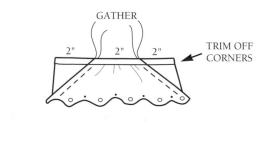

GATHER

2"   2"   2"

TRIM OFF CORNERS

4. Baste lace from binding to edge of lace, pull thread to gather both ends. Cut two 7" lengths of 7/8" wide ribbon. Place one edge of ribbon over edge of lace insert 1/4"; ribbon should come to dot C at center of lace insert in front, and 1/4" from center back of back bodice. Topstitch ribbon to bodice, near edge of ribbon.

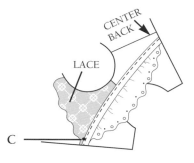

CENTER BACK

LACE

C

5. Slip gathered lace right side up under free edge of ribbon, having ends of lace 3/8" from raw edge of bodice, and hiding bound and gathered edge of lace under ribbon. Topstitch near edge of ribbon to hold lace in. Repeat for other side of the dress.

CENTER BACK

C

6. Sew remaining front bodice to remaining shoulder seams of back bodices.

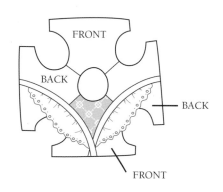

FRONT

BACK

BACK

FRONT

7. Bring plain front bodice down over lace front bodice, matching all raw edges, right sides together. Bodice backs will fold in half along center back. Stitch around neck hole. Clip to stitching every 1/2", turn right side out, and press.

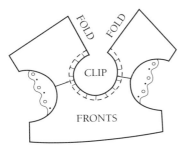

FOLD FOLD

CLIP

FRONTS

8. Pin gathered sleeve top to armhole opening, right sides together, sew. Be careful to keep lace out of seam. Repeat for other sleeve.

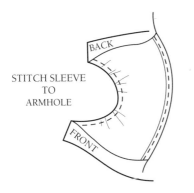

BACK

STITCH SLEEVE
TO
ARMHOLE

FRONT

9. Fold sleeve in half lengthwise, right sides together, matching underarm seams. Sew from sleeve hem, being careful to not catch string, to lower edge of bodice. Repeat for other underarm and side seam.

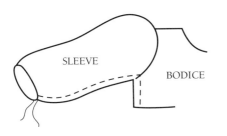

SLEEVE

BODICE

10. Press a fold, wrong sides together, in skirt 1 3/4" up from one long edge. Sew 1/8" from fold to form a pin tuck on right side of fabric. Press a second fold 3/4" away,

closer to raw edge. Sew again 1/8" from fold. Using a narrow hemming foot, hem lower edge or turn up 1/8" twice and sew. Turn short edges of skirt to wrong side 1/4" and sew. Baste upper edge of skirt and gather to fit lower edge of bodice. Sew right sides together, treating both layers of bodice as one piece. *Note:* Slip may be gathered with skirt and sewn in one seam to the bodice top. Tie bow in 7/8" ribbon and tack at center front. Make two horizontal buttonholes in left back bodice 1/4" from top and 1/4" up from skirt seam. Sew buttons to other bodice back 1/4" from edge.

To make slip: Narrowly hem or serge sides and lower edge of slip. Topstitch 4" lace to lower edge. Turn top edge of slip down 1/2" to form casing over string or ribbon (as you did on sleeve ends). Turn under ends of lace and sew to finish off raw edges. Tie on bunny just under arms.

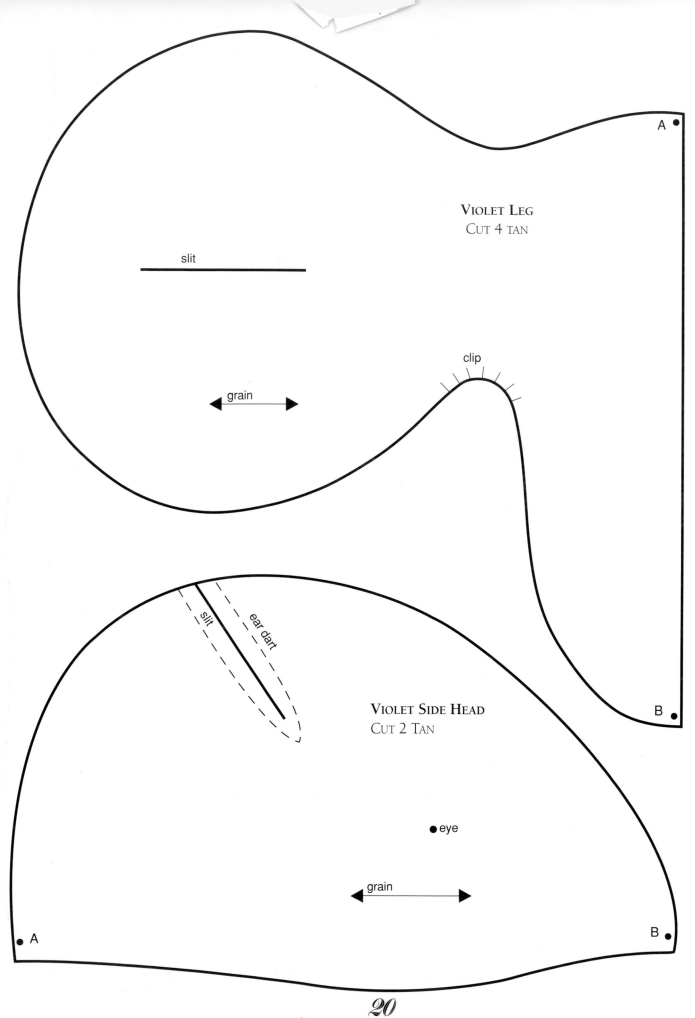

VIOLET LEG
CUT 4 TAN

slit

grain

clip

A

B

slit

ear dart

VIOLET SIDE HEAD
CUT 2 TAN

eye

grain

A

B

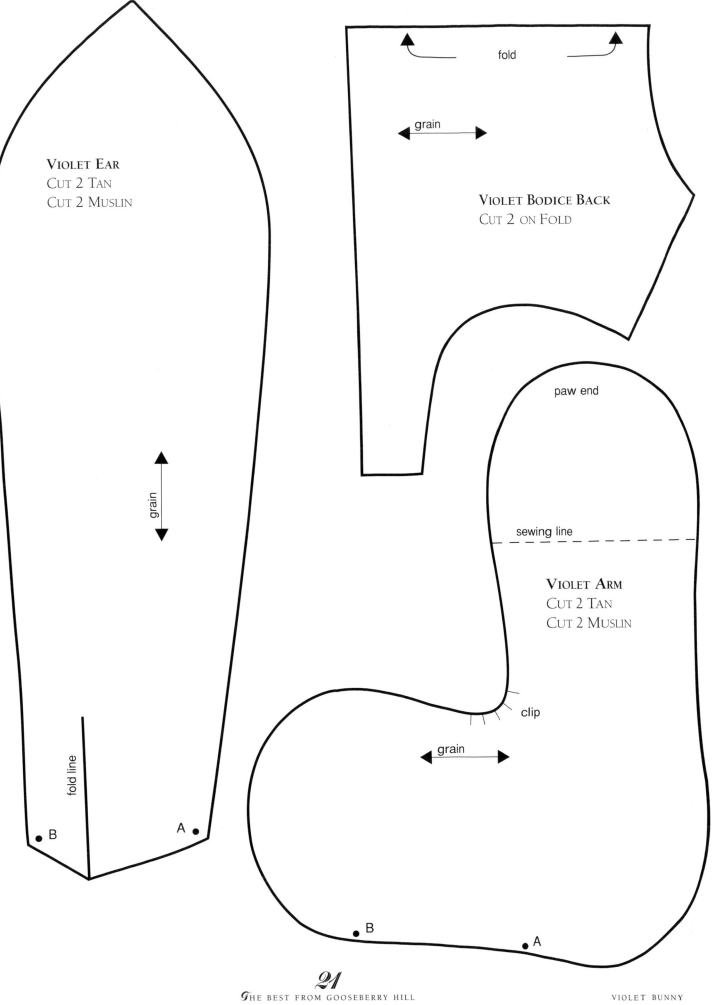

VIOLET EAR
CUT 2 TAN
CUT 2 MUSLIN

grain

fold line

B

A

VIOLET BODICE BACK
CUT 2 ON FOLD

fold

grain

paw end

sewing line

VIOLET ARM
CUT 2 TAN
CUT 2 MUSLIN

clip

grain

B

A

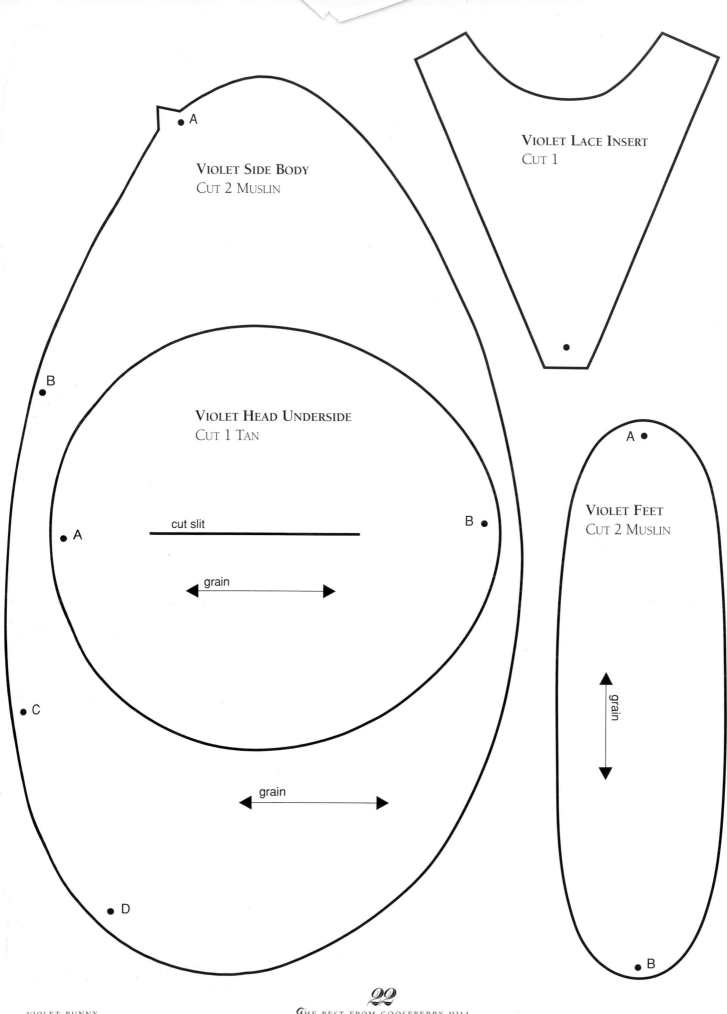

VIOLET SIDE BODY
CUT 2 MUSLIN

A

B

VIOLET HEAD UNDERSIDE
CUT 1 TAN

A

cut slit

grain

B

C

grain

D

VIOLET LACE INSERT
CUT 1

VIOLET FEET
CUT 2 MUSLIN

A

grain

B

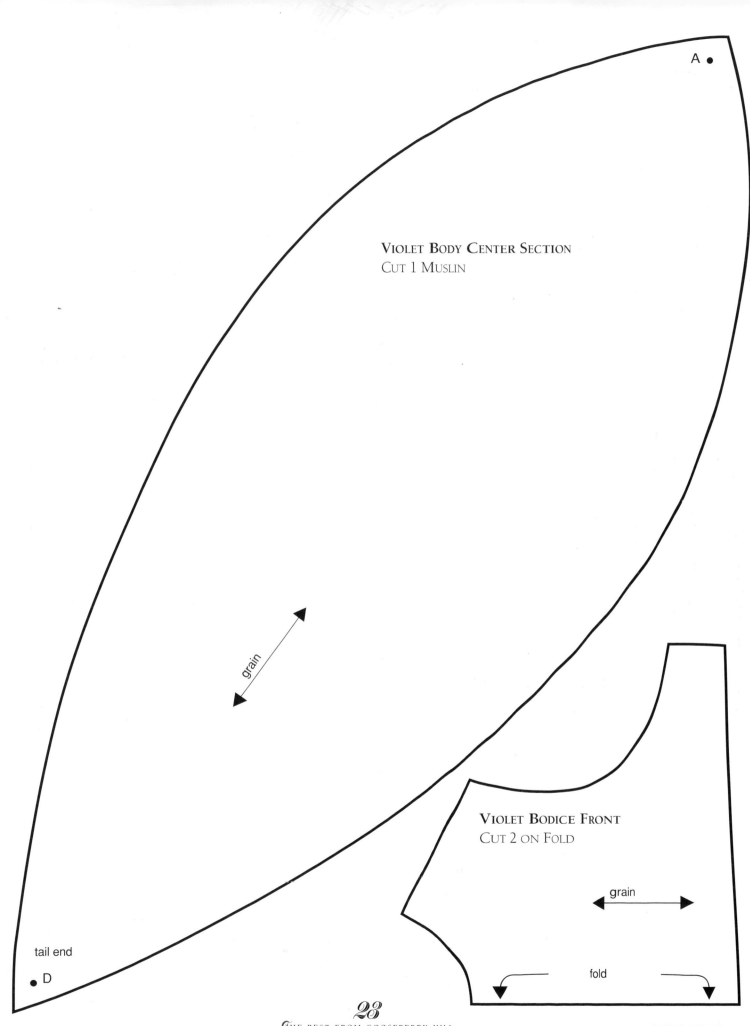

VIOLET BODY CENTER SECTION
CUT 1 MUSLIN

A •

grain

VIOLET BODICE FRONT
CUT 2 ON FOLD

grain

fold

tail end

• D

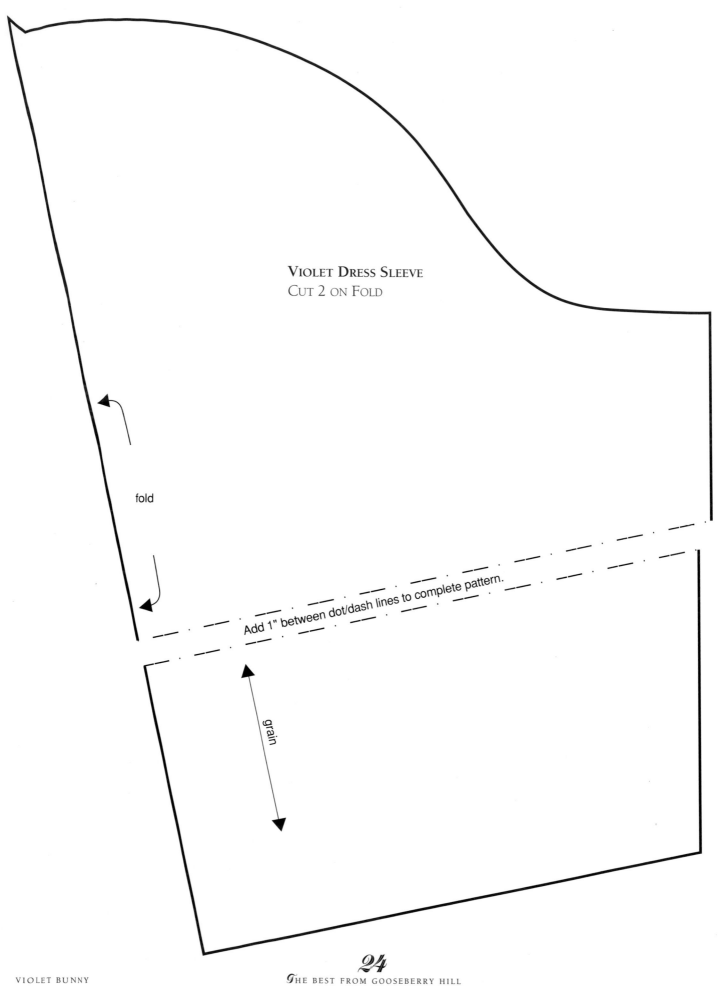

VIOLET DRESS SLEEVE
CUT 2 ON FOLD

fold

Add 1" between dot/dash lines to complete pattern.

grain

To Rebecca the lengths of brown gingham were interminable. She made hard work of sewing, broke the thread, dropped her thimble into the syringa bushes, pricked her finger, wiped the perspiration from her forehead, could not match the checks, puckered the seams. She polished her needles to nothing, pushing them in and out of the emery strawberry, but they always squeaked. Still Aunt Jan's patience held good, and some small measure of skill was creeping into Rebecca's fingers, fingers that held pencil, paint brush, and pen so cleverly and were so clumsy with the dainty little needle.

≈

—Kate Douglas Wiggin
Rebecca of Sunnybrook Farm, 1903.

LITTLE SEWING ANGEL

©1993 Kathy Pace

We always try to attend the annual Fall antique show in the Salt Lake Valley. Once, I found a little sailor sewing dolly, made entirely of felt, lying among assorted other little sewing tools. I'm always interested in old sewing things. As I looked at her, I wondered if she was a gift to someone taking a cruise, or even if she might have been a clever way to present a useful sewing kit to guests on a steam liner. The layers of felt were simply glued together. She wasn't stuffed like the dolly presented here. She had spools of thread on her legs and an extra layer of felt for needles, like my angel dolly. Safety pins were hidden under her blouse and there was a piece of elastic on her back to hold a little pair of scissors. She was a complete emergency sewing kit, as useful as she was pretty.

Our sewing friends always enjoy little gifts that can be given to members of their quilting circle or needlework club. This little cherub is a great gift for anyone, sewer or not. She would be adorable in Christmas fabrics or dressed to match any room decor. It would be fun to sew all white buttons around the edge of her pinafore or along her dress hem. A special monogram could be added to her pinafore front or stitched on the heart wings before you put the two halves together. A pretty decorative stitch could be done in a contrasting color instead of the plain topstitching on her pinafore. Her hair could be changed to match the recipient's hair and the halo removed to make a more personalized gift.

This little angel is just the right size to tuck into a suit-case or overnight kit, and she's guaranteed to cheer the weary traveler.

Cutting Instructions: Pattern pieces are on pages 30-31. Cut two heads, two bodies, two legs, one arm from tan fabric. Cut one pinafore and four heart wings from white fabric. Cut one sleeve and one skirt from striped fabric. Cut two heart wings from interfacing. Cut one piece of braid hair 2" long and one piece 1" long.

SUPPLY LIST

1/8 yd. tan fabric for body

3" braided doll hair

1 1/4 yds. gathered 1/2" lace

1/4 yd. interfacing

1/8 yd. striped fabric

1/4 yd. white fabric

Small amount of stuffing

Brown embroidery floss

1/2 yd. of 1/4" elastic

Matching threads

1/2 yd. of 1/2" ribbon for sash

1/3 yd. of 1/4" ribbon for scissors tie

Tacky Glue

Two white shirt buttons

Thin gold cord or thread

Red pen

Powdered blush

Cotton swabs

String or strong thread

Small square of white felt

Two small safety pins

Two medium thimbles

One 1/2" heart button

One large spool of thread to put on legs

1a. Cut slit in one head piece as indicated. Mark eyes and mouth on other head piece. With right sides together, sew heads all around the outside edge. Trim seam allowance and turn right side out. Stuff and whipstitch opening closed. Make French knots for eyes using six strands of embroidery floss and only wrapping once around the needle. Tie off behind the head.

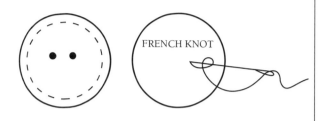

For the French knot eyes: Come up at eye dot, wrap the thread around the needle, hold wrapped thread near fabric, pull the needle through eye dot to the back of the head.

1b. Gently untwist 1" braid hair and glue to top of the head at the back so it hangs down and covers the back of the head.

1c. Gently separate 2" piece of braid hair and glue over top of head covering raw ends of 1" piece previously glued. Sew two shirt buttons to head to hold hair like barrettes. (Hide knots for shirt button thread on back of head.) Tie a gold thread around forehead if desired. Make three dots with a red pen for mouth. Twist a cotton swab in powder blush and twirl on each cheek for blush. Set head aside.

2a. Sew two legs together from A to B leaving top open. Trim seam allowance, turn right side out, stuff lower half of leg. Repeat for the other leg.

2b. Sew 4" elastic loop to top of leg. Repeat for the other leg.

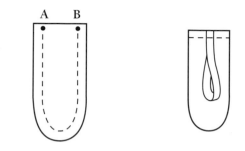

2c. Sew legs (elastic side down) to one body.

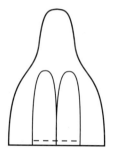

2d. Fold legs down, place other body on top of body with legs. Sew from A to B leaving lower edge with legs open. Clip and trim seam allowances, turn right side out, stuff, and whipstitch opening closed.

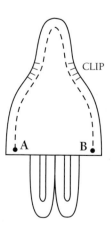

3. Fold arms on fold line. Sew from A to B and C to D. Trim seam allowances, turn right side out, and stuff ends only for about 1". Whipstitch opening closed.

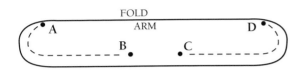

4a. Hem short edges of sleeves with a narrow turn-under allowance. On wrong side, stretch and sew on a 2 1/2" piece of 1/4" elastic 1/2" from both edges, using a zigzag stitch. (It is easier to use a long piece of elastic and cut off the excess than to try to cut and handle a tiny piece.)

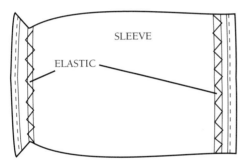

4b. Fold sleeve right sides together. Sew across lower edge. Turn right side out. Slip onto arms.

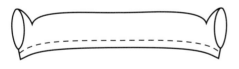

4c. Tie off center of arms tightly with a strong thread or string.

5a. Hem three edges of skirt with a narrow turn-under allowance.

5b. Gather the top edge to fit around top of body. Leave 3/4" of neck exposed. Tie tightly to body using string.

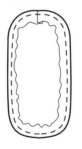

6a. Sew lace to right side of pinafore near bound edge of lace. Overlap ends of lace at the back.

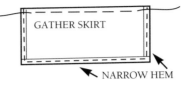

6b. Turn seam to wrong side and press. Topstitch 1/8" from seam on right side to hold lace in place. With felt piece on wrong side of pinafore and lower edges even, sew across top of felt 1/4" from end. (This piece of felt is for needles.)

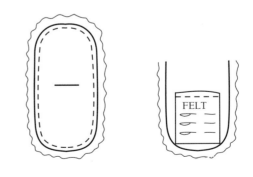

Directions continue on page 32.

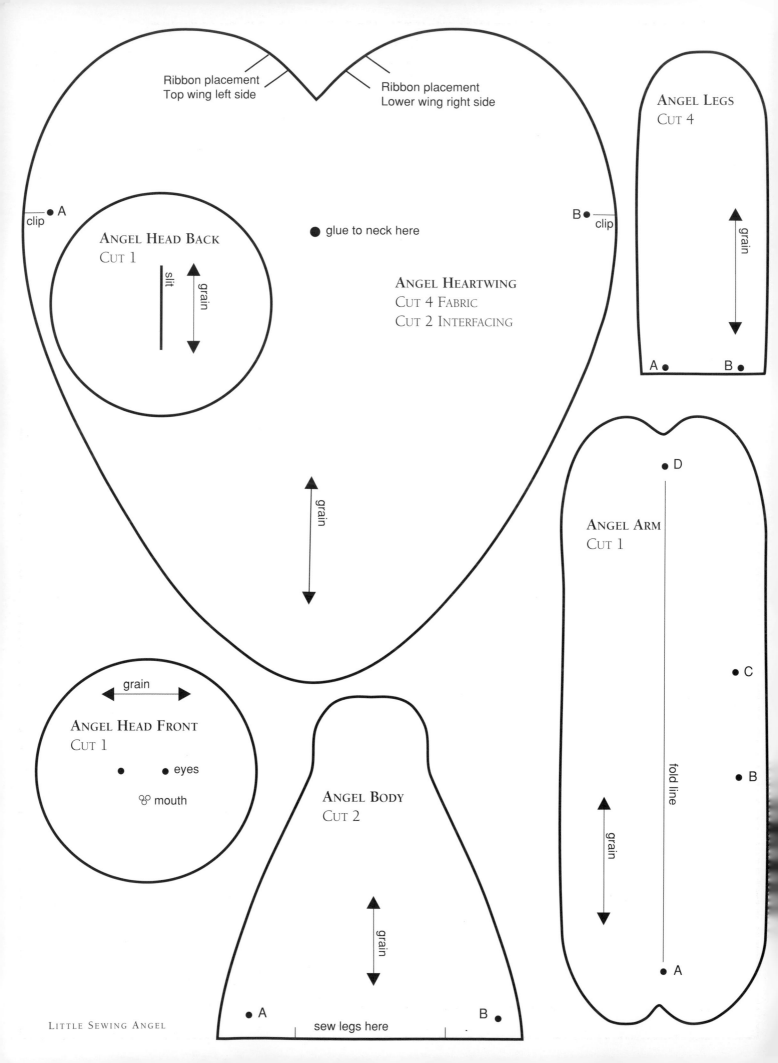

Ribbon placement
Top wing left side

Ribbon placement
Lower wing right side

ANGEL LEGS
CUT 4

grain

● A

clip

ANGEL HEAD BACK
CUT 1

slit

grain

B ●

clip

● glue to neck here

ANGEL HEARTWING
CUT 4 FABRIC
CUT 2 INTERFACING

A ●   B ●

grain

● D

ANGEL ARM
CUT 1

● C

fold line

grain   grain   ● B

ANGEL HEAD FRONT
CUT 1

● ● eyes

⅋ mouth

ANGEL BODY
CUT 2

grain

● A

LITTLE SEWING ANGEL

● A   ● B

sew legs here

● A

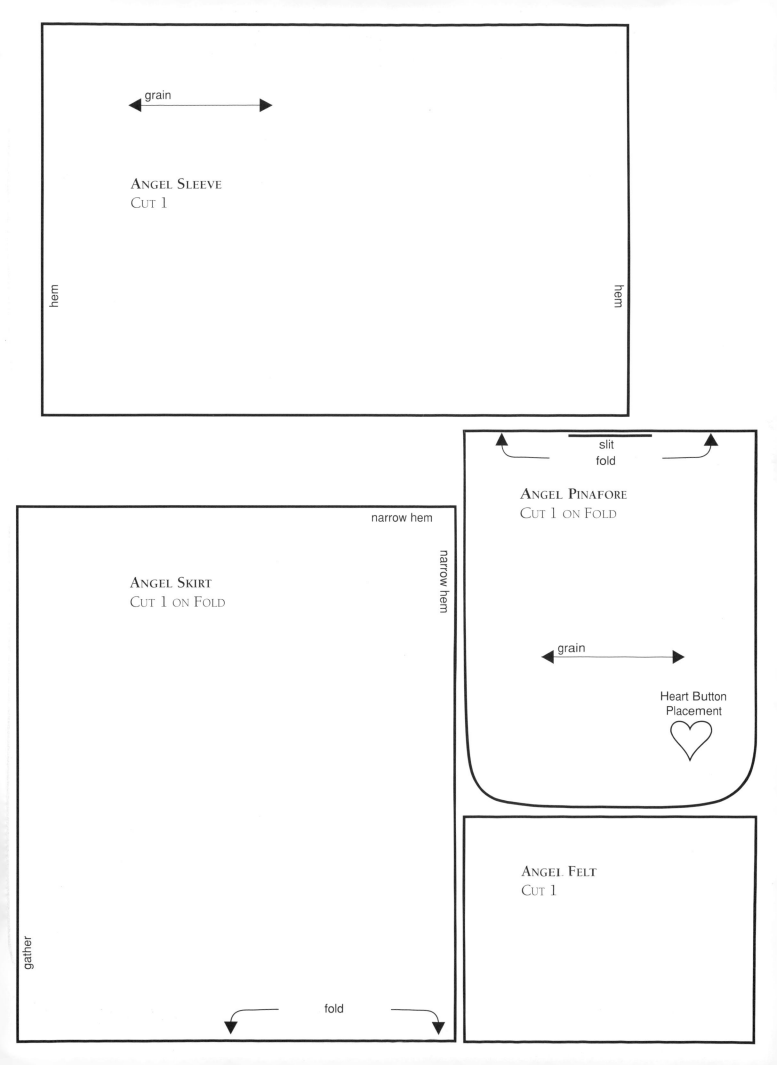

7a. Layer one fabric heart wing, right side up, on top of interfacing. Sew lace to top of heart wing from A to B, turning ends of lace under 1/4". Cut 1/4"-wide ribbon into two 6" pieces. Sew ribbon to heart as illustrated. Repeat for second heart wing.

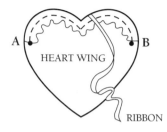

7b. Place second fabric heart on top of first, right sides together. Sew from A to B. Clip as indicated to dots A and B and all around top of hearts. Turn right side out and press. Repeat steps A and B for the second heart wing. Then place one on top of the other.

7c. Sew from A to B around the pointed end of the heart. Turn right side out and place scissors inside. Tie ribbon through a scissors handle.

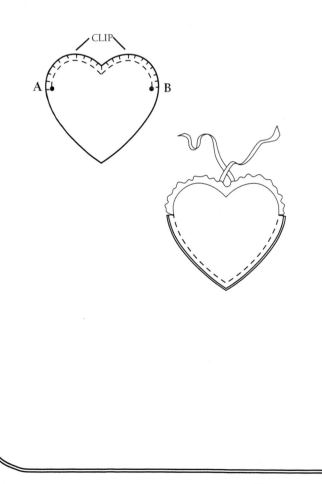

8. Glue arms at top of skirt on front of body. Put pinafore on with neck coming out through the slit. Glue head on top of neck. Tie pinafore on with a wide ribbon. Part hair at back so neck is exposed. Glue heart wings to back of neck. Push sleeves up and pin a safety pin to each hand. Push thimbles onto feet. Put a spool of thread into leg elastics. Sew heart button near left corner of pinafore. Enjoy!

Tapestry Goose

Simple lines make this 12" goose an elegant accent piece for the table or mantle, and it looks great nestled in a basket. Try velvet, chintz or calico fabrics to change decorating styles. Project time is just one hour.

Violet Bunny

Precious Violet is truly a bunny to love. She sits 12" tall and has an easy, glue-together body. Instructions for her Victorian dress with its doily, ribbon, and lace-trimmed yoke are included.

Sewing Bird Pincushion

This sweet little 4" bird will bring happiness to your heart. Several will look great on a Christmas tree or wreath, or in a basket, and they make darling gifts for friends who sew.

Turkey Gobbler

Here's the perfect centerpiece for fall! Our turkey is 11½" tall and has a gathered-ruffle fan tail trimmed with yards of eyelet lace. His head is easily appliquéd onto the body, and the wings are quilted and trimmed with a narrow ruffle and lace.

Rosebud Bear

Rosebud is an adorable 12" tall bear that can be finished in a day. She is fully jointed, and her head even turns. The bears shown here are made with European distressed mohair, a natural wool fur. Be careful: Bear making can be habit forming!

Little Sewing Angel

Beautiful as well as functional, this little cherub is really a neat little sewing kit disguised as a dolly. In her clothes, you'll find safety pins, a felt square for needle storage, a spool of thread, thimbles, scissors, and extra shirt buttons.

Our Old-Fashioned Elf

Here is a Christmas charmer who looks wonderful sitting on a shelf, under the Christmas tree, or even in a wreath. He is 19" tall, and all of his clothes are included in the pattern.

Father Christmas

This Santa is truly Victorian. He stands 24" tall and has a simple rag-doll body. His coat is topped off with a crazy-quilted cape embellished with stitching, beads, buttons, braids, and charms.

The power, which resides in man, is new in nature, and none but he knows what that is which he can do nor does he know until he has tried.

—Ralph Waldo Emerson

～

That lies behind us and what lies before us are tiny matters compared to what lies within us.

—Oliver Wendell Holmes

TURKEY GOBBLER

©1982 Kathy Pace

The Turkey Gobbler was one of my earliest patterns. I was sewing in a corner of our basement bedroom with a little wood-burning stove nearby. I used paper grocery bags opened out flat for pattern paper, and I used old fabrics from my mother's collection to make the prototypes, to make sure I had the body shape right. When I finally had the design perfected, it was time for bed. I still remember the vivid dreams I had that night of the finished turkey in his rust, creams, and browns. He was so beautiful that I was too excited to wait even one day. As soon as we awoke, I piled the kids into the van and drove to Salt Lake City to get the dream fabrics.

Those colors were popular for home decor at that time. I think it still makes a nice fall centerpiece in those colors, with Indian corn, gourds, pumpkins, cornstalk tassels, and wheat sheaves.

However, if you'd like to try something new, how about using the colors of your room decor? Once I made a turkey from a black fabric that had mauve and white roses. The fabric had a border print with a stripe that looked wonderful on the tail, and I used mauve solid for the piping and wattle; the lace was white. I now like the ruffles a little wider, so new dimensions are included in this version of the pattern.

I never liked putting the safety eyes in during the sewing process: Sometimes the sewing or stuffing made the eyes come out unevenly. It was funny to see how different the turkey could look, depending on where the eyes were placed. So I used hot glue to place the turkey eyes. (It is important to keep these turkeys away from small children; glued-on eyes can be easily bitten off for a small snack.)

SUPPLY LIST

1/2 yd. (45" wide) wide-striped fabric

1/4 yd. narrow-striped fabric

1/8 yd. rust-colored fabric (for head)

1/2 yd. brown print (for body)

1 1/3 yds. medium to heavy-weight iron on interfacing

Beige felt (for beak)

1/3 yd. of 1/4"-diameter poly cord

3 1/3 yds. of 1 1/4" gathered beige eyelet lace

Rust-colored machine embroidery or regular thread

Brown thread

Two small pieces batting (for wing padding)

Two 8mm round eyes

12 oz. polyester stuffing

Heavy duty sewing machine needle

Cutting Instructions: All pattern pieces will be found on the pull-out pages at the back of this book. Cut one breast, two tails, two side bodies and four wings from brown fabric. Cut two wattles and two heads from rust color fabric. Cut four wing-tip ruffles from wide stripe fabric. Cut two beak pieces from beige felt. No patterns are given for the following: From wide-striped fabric, cut two 6" wide x 45" long strips and one pieced for piping 2" wide x 15 1/2" long. From narrow-striped fabric, cut two narrow strips 3" x 36".

1. Take one head and pin it to a side body piece, matching notches on both pieces right sides up. Lay them on a piece of typing paper, loosen upper machine tension and use machine embroidery thread or regular sewing thread for the upper thread. Set machine to widest satin stitch (wide, close zigzag) and set the forward movement about where you would set it for button holes. With the piece of typing paper under the fabrics, machine appliqué the lower raw edge of the head to the body with the satin stitch. Repeat for the other head and side body. Re-tighten upper tension and switch to regular straight stitch. Rip away excess paper.

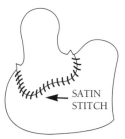

SATIN STITCH

2a. Place two wings right sides together on top of a piece of batting and stitch from dot A around the wing to dot B through all thicknesses. Pivot the needle at dots between wing feathers (see pattern piece). Clip all curves. Clip at slash marks between feathers on pattern piece. Turn right side out. Use a pencil eraser or closed scissors to completely turn feather points out. Use regular straight stitch and sew through all thicknesses to machine quilt along feather lines. Repeat for other wing. Put two wing tip ruffles right sides together. Pin 1 1/4"-wide gathered eyelet lace between the two pieces, with the bound edge of lace close to the raw edges of the fabric beginning at dot C and ending at dot D going along long curved edge. Stitch with a slightly wider than 1/4" seam from C around to D. Turn right side out and press. Gather straight edge of the ruffle until it is about 5" long. Pin to underside of wing so it extends out from feather tips. Topstitch from right side of wing beginning at edge of one feather and going across all the feather tips as shown. Repeat for other wing.

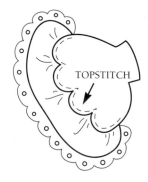

TOPSTITCH

2b. To attach wing to body, transfer dots on side body pattern to side body fabric. Lay wing with right side next to right side of body, match dot A to A and B to B and sew through all layers from A to B. Then, fold wing down to normal position. *Note:* Longer wing feather is lowest. Repeat for other wing and side body.

STITCH

3. Stitch two bodies right sides together from notch on head around back to dot E. Clip curves. Stitch two tail pieces right sides together across the top only, from dot F to dot G. Clip curves.

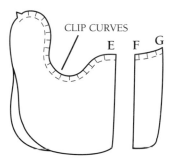

CLIP CURVES   E   F   G

4. To make side piping: cut 1/4" poly cord to 12" long. Lay cord in center of wrong side of 2" wide strip. Fold strip over cord. Using a zipper foot, sew as close to the cord as you can. Let fabric extend over both ends of cord. Sew straight off both ends of fabric, even though the cord doesn't guide you at the ends.

5. To make wide tail ruffle, cut heavy-weight iron on interfacing to fit one of the 6" x 45" long strips of wide stripe fabric. Iron it to the wrong side of one piece. Lay the two 6" x 45" strips right sides together and trim off one corner on each end as shown. As with wing tip ruffles, put lace between strips with bound edge of lace even with raw edges of long curved edge of ruffle, stitch. Clip curves and turn right side out. Topstitch 1/8" from edge of fabric along lace edge. Mark center of ruffle with a pin. Gather straight edge to measure 13 1/2". Tie threads so the gathering won't slip. Set aside. Iron interfacing to the wrong side of one narrow stripe strip (3" x 36"). Lay two 3" x 36" strips right sides together and

trim off one corner on each end as you did for the wide ruffle. Put lace between, stitch, clip, turn, topstitch, mark center, gather and tie off, the same as for the ruffle you've just finished.

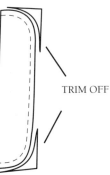

TRIM OFF

6. Open out body section flat, center and pin piping made in step 4 on top of right side of body's back edge with raw edges even. Using zipper foot, stitch as close to piping as you can.

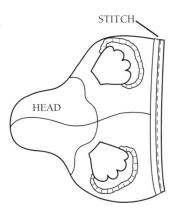

STITCH

HEAD

Adjust gathers on narrow ruffle and pin narrow stripe ruffle on top of piping with gathered raw edges even with raw edges of piping and center of ruffle on center back seam. Still using the zipper foot, sew through ruffle with needle as close to piping as you can get. *Note:* The ends of the ruffle should not come to the edges of the side body. Don't let the ruffle extend beyond dot H at either end. Use a heavy-duty size 16 needle.

Pin the wide ruffle on top of the narrow ruffle, centers matching, and pin the opened-out tail section right side down on top of it, matching notches. It may be easier to turn the whole thing over now and with the body on top, sew through all thicknesses from dot J to dot J along previous stitching line. Continue to use zipper foot and sew as close to piping as possible. Finger press all seam allowances toward front of turkey. If desired, topstitch next to piping through body and all seam allowances to keep them pulled forward. Otherwise, the tail has a tendency to flop forward.

7. Pin breast to one side body matching dots G on breast and tail, and dots A on head and breast, right sides together. Carefully keep tail and wing feathers out of the

way. Stitch from dot G around body to dot A at head using 1/4" seam, and leaving an opening between dots H and I so you will be able to turn and stuff.

Carefully bunch the tail ruffles and wings together and pin the free edge of the breast section to the free edge of the body right sides together. Ease the curves so they come out even and stitch again from tail's dot G down the side you just pinned and up past notch on head. When you come to the end of the breast section, at dot A, take a slightly deeper seam allowance so there won't be a hole there when he is turned right side out. You should now have a completed turkey shape inside out.

Clip curves and turn right side out very carefully. Stuff head and neck and breast very tightly. Stuff tail tightly, especially at base so the gobbler won't rock backward with weight of his tail fathers. Stuff middle of back so it has a nice arch and fill in center last. The tighter you stuff it, the nicer it will look. Pin and blind stitch opening closed.

8a. For beak, fold upper beak in half wrong sides together and topstitch 1/8" from fold. Top stitching will be on outside of finished beak. Open upper beak out flat with ridge up. Place lower beak on top of it, right sides together. Matching dots, sew from M to L to N using 1/8" seam. Turn right side out. Pin two wattles right sides together. Stitch leaving open between two dots to turn. Clip curves. Use a pencil eraser to turn right side out. If the pencil gets stuck, use a toothpick to finish pushing it inside out. Rub it between your fingers to work it into the finished shape.

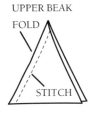

UPPER BEAK

FOLD

STITCH

8b. Glue or hand tack the open end of wattle under the right side of top of beak then fold wattle across nose to opposite side and glue there. Let it hang freely down below beak. Hand stitch or glue beak to head. See picture on page 42 for approximate beak placement. Sew or glue eyes in place. Sew or glue wing to back in a couple of places so it won't flap around.

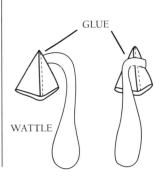

GLUE

WATTLE

ROSEBUD BEAR

For years I've loved the antique bears that I've seen at doll and bear shows and featured in country magazines. They look so adorable piled in an old trunk or sitting on a bed. There can't be anything more appealing than a little bear with his fur loved off in spots and a shaggy, lumpy body. The major fault of old bears is the prohibitive price tag: some of the really wonderful ones start at $100 for every inch of height! Bears have sold at auctions for much more. At those prices, a buggy full of old bears would cost a king's ransom. So, the solution is to make our own bears.

A friend introduced me to distressed mohair a few years ago. It looks just like the bears made early in this century. It is even twisted and flattened and has bare spots where the backing shows through. When it is made into a bear, he already looks old and love-worn. We trim more fur off his nose area, leaving a 1/8" stubble to simulate the real wear on an old bear. When the first shipment of mohair came in, I made forty bears as fast as I could sew. Every time I made a bear out of a new color or length of fur, it would look so different from all the others that I could hardly believe my eyes. It is difficult to make two bears look alike, even when you try. Each seems to take on his own interesting personality as you stuff and stitch. Also, long fur and large ears make a fluffy, younger-looking bear, while shorter furs and small ears make the bears seem more grown-up.

Modern bears with sewn-in legs just don't have the old-fashioned appeal that jointed bears have. Some people have commented that making a jointed teddy bear looks difficult because they don't know how to put the joints together. But it's really very simple.

The only joints that I knew about at first were the plastic doll joints. I was never very happy with them because, no matter how tightly they were pressed together, the bear would flop over because the joints were too loose. I am much happier with the cotter-pin joints, which are available from a hardware store. Instructions for these joints are included here. If you have difficulty in finding the mohair, we carry both yardage and kits complete with 100% wool felt for the bears' paw pads and the joints we like the best. Buying the mohair is an investment in heirloom quality. The bear will be beautiful 100 years from now. Compared to the price of an antique bear, it is very inexpensive. Now the buggy full of bears is affordable.

Bears are so popular that they have become a large part of our business: I designed a family with Napoleon, Camille, and Wee Bears as the Papa, Mama, and Baby bears. Our Elegant Stocking pattern contains a jointed bear only 5" tall. I really wanted to do a pattern that looked just like an antique bear that I have from Germany, dated approximately 1903, and I obtained permission from the manufacturer in the spring of 1991. I named him simply 1903 Bear. He is very true to the old styling; he even has a hump on his back like the original. The ears are hand-sewn to the head after finishing, so they have the perfect curve to them. This 16" tall bear has the long arms and big feet that make the old bears so charming. Rosebud is the little sister to 1903 Bear. She uses only one-fourth yard of mohair, yet she still turns out to be a very cute and plump bear of 12".

There were old bears made out of pink fur at one point in time. We thought it would be fun to show this little bear in pink, since the fur is so beautiful. She also looks wonderful in the tans and beiges of the earlier bears. Although I do love and recommend mohair fabric, all of our bears can be made from fake fur. Just be sure to choose a short nap of 3/8" to 1/2". The thinner furs with soft backings make good bears; long fur hides the shape of the head.

Supply List

1/4 yd. distressed mohair or short pile
(1/2" or less) thin fake fur

Five pair 1 1/2" joints

4" x 6" of cream colored felt

Two 12mm safety eyes

Gray or light brown perle cotton

1 cup plastic weighted pellets

1 yd. 1" wired ribbon for neck

16 oz. polyfil stuffing

Dental floss

Matching thread

Note: No pattern is given for Rosebud Bear's dress.

Cutting Instructions: Pattern pieces are on pages 51-53. Fold fur in half the long way with fur side in. Cut out pieces from fur and felt as directed on pattern pieces. The arrows showing fur direction are just a suggestion.

ROSEBUD CUTTING LAYOUT

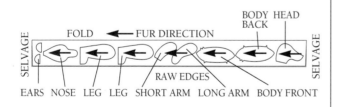

A Word on Joints: I found the cotter pin/disc joints to be the easiest to use, and the tightest. Plastic joints aren't as tight as the cotter pin/disc joints, and tend to loosen up as the fur in the joint area wears down, but they are quick. Both joints are illustrated here. You can apply my directions to any form of the joint, shank being the term used to describe the part of the joint that goes from arm, leg, or head into the body, whether it be cotter pin, or plastic.

PLASTIC JOINT

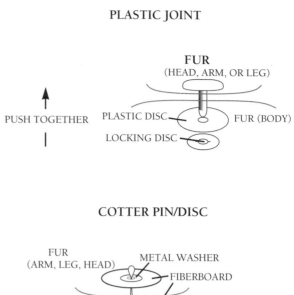

COTTER PIN/DISC

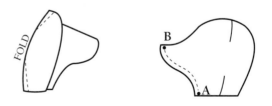

1a. Fold head right sides together. Sew ear and neck darts in head. Repeat for other head.

1b. Sew two heads together from A to B right sides together.

1c. Carefully pin nose to heads, right sides together, matching notch B (nose) to dot B (head). Lower edge C's should match. Sew where pinned.

2a. Sew two ears right sides together from A to B. Trim off corners, turn right side out, fold raw edges inside and whipstitch opening closed. Repeat for other ear pieces.

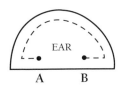

EAR
A   B

2b. Put safety eyes in at dots. Stuff head firmly, putting extra into nose and cheek area. Leave 1/2" of neck unstuffed.

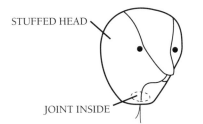

STUFFED HEAD

JOINT INSIDE

2c. Baste around lower edge of head 3/8" from raw edge with two strands of dental floss. Begin with a 10" tail and take long stitches (3/8"). Leave a tail 10" long. Place plastic snap in joint, or disc with washer and cotter pin, inside head. (Pin or shank sticks out.) Draw up basting thread (dental floss) so raw edges of fabric just touch shank. Then knot thread ends, backstitch, and trim off.

3. Use a brush or needle to pull fur out of the seam in the head. *Optional:* Clip off fur 1/4" away from seams at nose. I trimmed more fur away from the head to make it look worn. Sew nose with one strand perle cotton. You can add a tiny piece of black felt under satin stitch of nose like shape indicated on illustration. To sew nose, bury a knot in face, satin stitch nose shape as shown. Stitch two long stitches for mouth. Go over mouth and nose again. Bury knot under edge of satin stitch and backstitch before tying off.

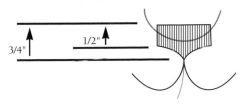

3/4"   1/2"

4a. Hand-sew ear to head with button thread or dental floss, starting 1/4" in front of ear dart on the head seam. Take a stitch in the head then a stitch through the ear. Pull tightly. Sew the ear to the seam for half of the ear. Then pull the ear down to touch the dart.

4b. Sew the ear to the head as before, and turn the bottom edge of the ear up slightly, along the dart. Tie off, backstitch, and clip excess thread. Repeat for other ear.

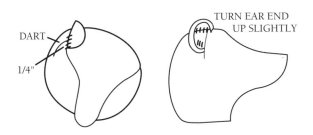

DART

1/4"

TURN EAR END UP SLIGHTLY

5a. Sew two backs together from D to E and F to G.

5b. Sew two fronts together from D to G.

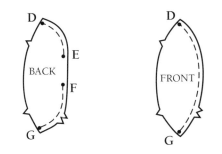

D
BACK
E
F
G

D
FRONT
G

5c. With double notch at bottom of front and double notch at bottom of back, place fronts and backs right sides together and pin. Match seams and notches. Sew all around, leaving a space of two stitches at D. Clip or poke joint holes in front of notches in fronts. Turn right side out. Joint head to body at D.

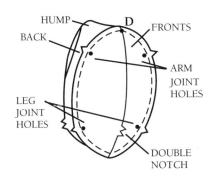

HUMP   D   FRONTS
BACK

ARM JOINT HOLES

LEG JOINT HOLES

DOUBLE NOTCH

6a. Sew leg from A to B and C to D. Clip at ankle. With legs lying opposite each other, mark and clip joint holes in one top layer of leg. Lightly mark hole location on fur side with pencil.

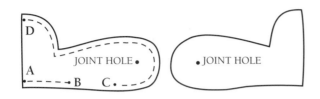

6b. Pin, then sew felt foot to opening, matching notches on foot to A and D on leg. Turn right side out, joint to body at leg notches, with toes pointing up. (Refer to general joint instructions in Step 7.)

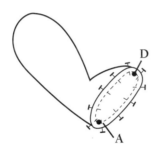

7a. Sew felt paw to short fur arm, matching notches and right sides together.

7b. Turn felt paw down and sew right sides together to long fur arm from A around to B. Clip inside curve. Clip joint hole on paw side of arm.

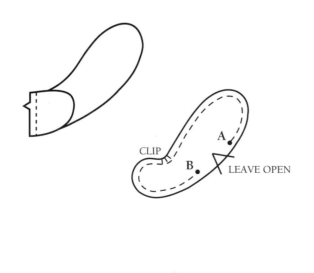

7c. Mark hole location on fur side as with leg. Turn right side out, joint to body with arms curving up.

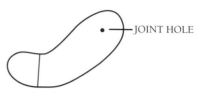

General Joint Instructions: Put a joint inside arm or leg with the shank sticking out of the hole. Put arm and leg and head shanks into body at correct holes. Inside the body place a disc and washer, or disc and locking disc over the shank. Then fasten joint.

Pour one cup of pellets into tummy. Finish stuffing body with polyfil stuffing. Stitch body closed. Stuff arms and legs with stuffing. Stitch openings closed. Tie wire ribbon in a bow around neck.

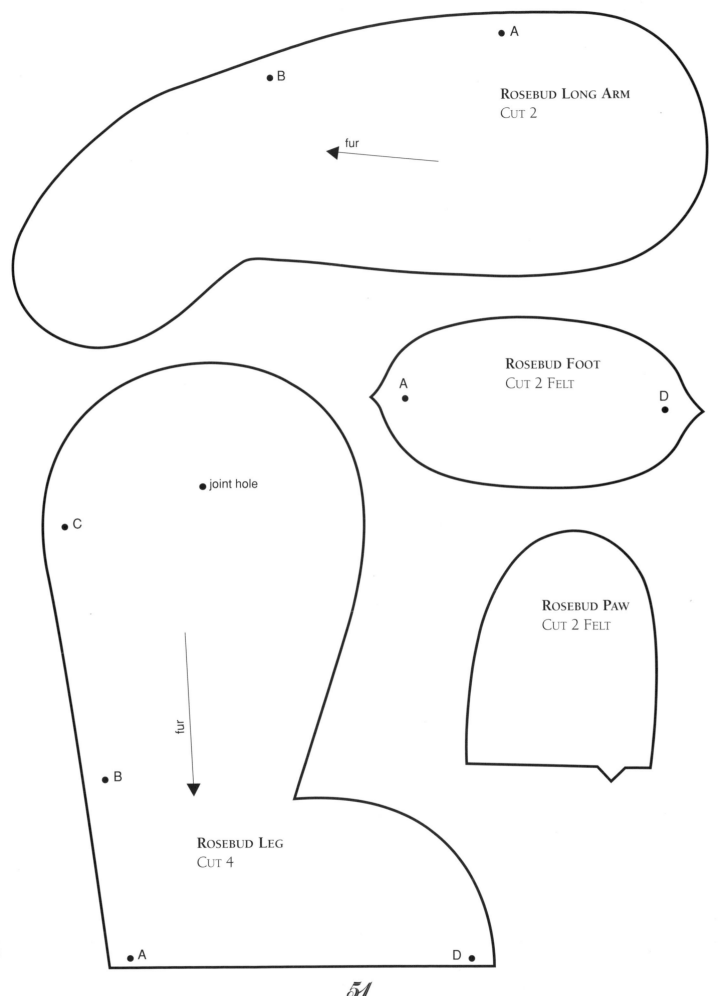

ROSEBUD LONG ARM
CUT 2

fur

ROSEBUD FOOT
CUT 2 FELT

A

D

• joint hole

• C

ROSEBUD PAW
CUT 2 FELT

fur

• B

ROSEBUD LEG
CUT 4

• A

D •

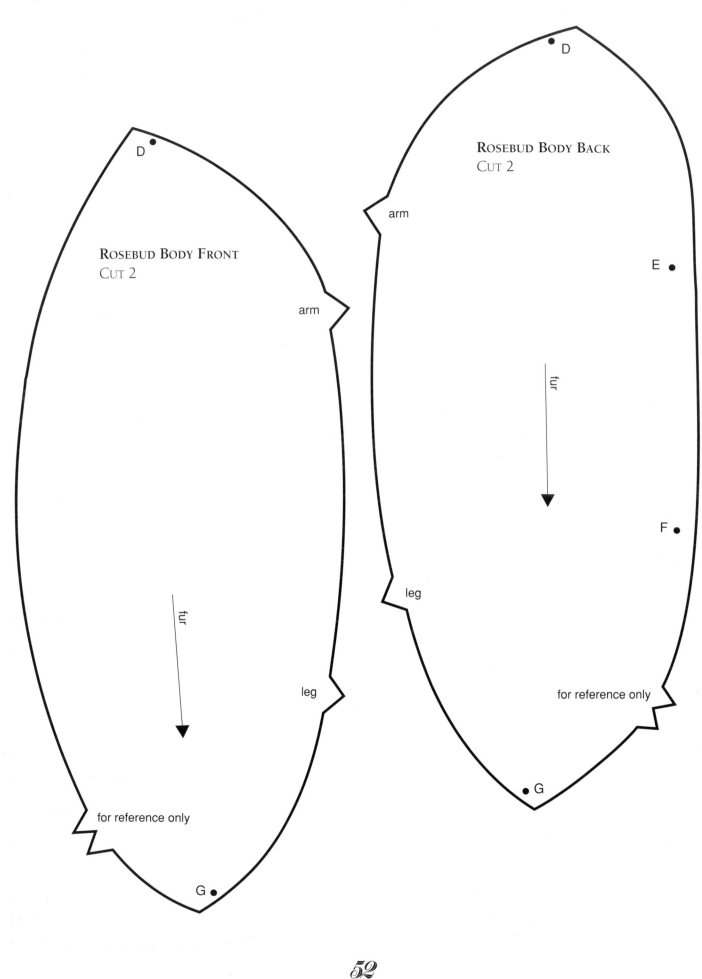

ROSEBUD BODY FRONT
CUT 2

D

arm

fur

leg

for reference only

G

ROSEBUD BODY BACK
CUT 2

D

arm

E

F

fur

leg

for reference only

G

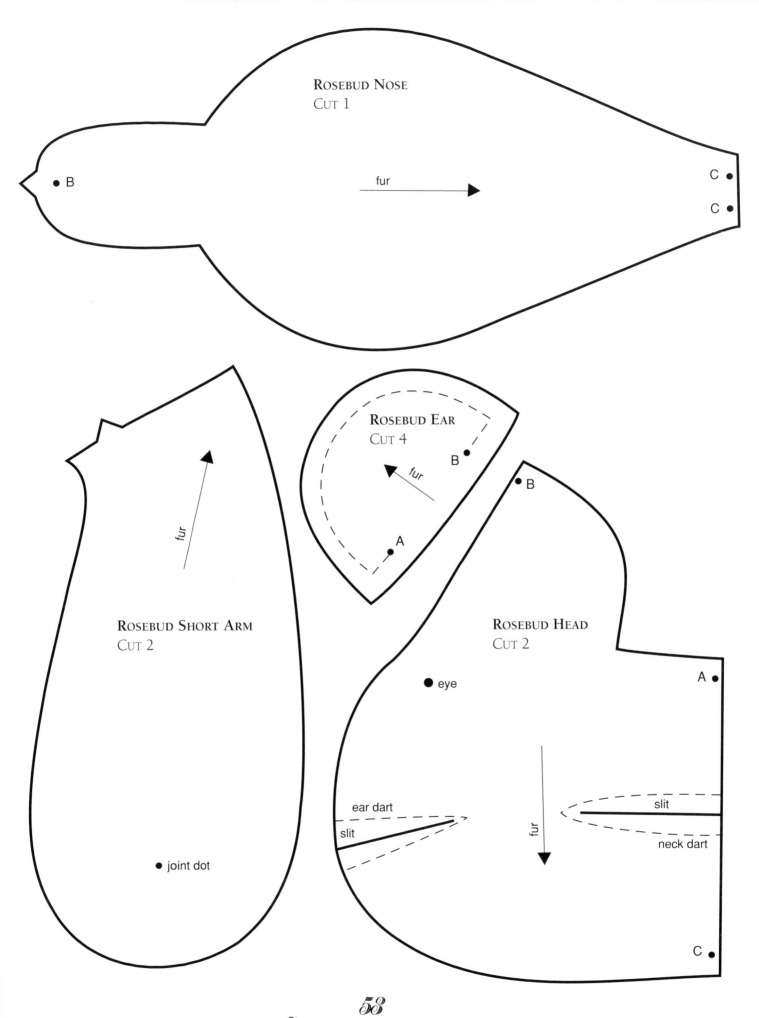

Rosebud Nose
Cut 1

• B

fur →

C •
C •

Rosebud Ear
Cut 4

B •

fur

A •

B •

Rosebud Short Arm
Cut 2

fur

• joint dot

Rosebud Head
Cut 2

• eye

A •

ear dart

slit

fur

slit

neck dart

C •

SEWING BIRD PINCUSHION

©1991 Kathy Pace

Did you ever have the feeling that you were being watched, turned around, and found you were? That is precisely what happened to me, and not once but several times a day, for several weeks during the spring of 1991. The eyes were small and bright, set in a tiny black face belonging to a curious bird. He perched on the back of the church pew on our front porch, as close to the sewing-room window as he could come. When I first discovered him, I wondered why he would gaze in at me. Birds often check out the log rafters for possible nesting sites, but just to sit and stare at a woman sewing? I couldn't figure him out at all. My ironing board is right by the window, but my ironing didn't scare him away either. I wondered if he thought that my button jars, which line the window sill, were filled with assorted seeds and berries. He was interested in something — he stayed and watched so often and for such a long time that it was a little unnerving.

It was early spring, and I was working hard to get my new line of patterns ready for Quilt Market in May. I really needed a fresh idea, and often gazed out of the window, hoping for inspiration. My inquisitive black-bird friend seemed to want me to notice him! He watched for my reaction as he turned this way and that, as if to say, "Look at this fine physique, at what a specimen I am!" Such noble lines, such a promising idea! That is when I grabbed a pencil and sketched a bird. At first I didn't know what I would use it for — maybe a Christmas ornament, or a basket decoration. But, as I worked on making it, the pins I had stuck near his tail reminded me of his pin feathers, and the little pincushion bird was formed. Of course scissors would be a great addition to make it a useful gift: I even tried to put the scissors through the head so the end of the scissors would form the beak, but that became too complicated, so I experimented until they nested where you see them.

You may not believe it, but as soon as I made my first stuffed bird, my live visitor lost interest in me and deserted his perch. I suspect he needed to make up for lost time in finding a lady friend who had a different interest in his fine physique. (If you ever visit Gooseberry Hill, you may see his calling card on the right end of the pew. When we washed and varnished the bench the next summer, I told my boys to leave the evidence to show to the nonbelievers.)

I want you to have fun and enjoy this bird, too. Choose a medium-sized print for the wings, breast, and tail. Roses, for example, that measure about 1" across are just right. Petite stripes and very small prints will also look pretty. After you have selected a print for the wings, select one of the colors from the print for the body of the bird. Solid colors, tone on tone, or very fine prints seem to look best on the head.

Once I made a bird out of an old linen runner, with the embroidered part on the sides of the body. I sewed old lace across the wings and, after the bird was finished, I added a cluster of old buttons to the wing, instead of just one to hold it in place.

Try putting a silk ribbon around the bird's neck (this one will definitely look feminine), tied in a bow with a rose and button cluster glued to the breast. A tiny straw bonnet trimmed with rosettes would look darling tied to her head.

If the bird is to be a gift, it would be especially lovely to tuck a beautiful pair of old (or reproduction) embroidery scissors under one wing. One wing tip could be fastened down with a snap, so it could be lifted to put needles in the wing underside. For a thimble carrier, weave narrow lace ribbon around the outer edge of a 3" or 4" doily. Pull the ribbon up around the thimble to form a little pouch. Tack the doily to a ribbon tied around the bird's neck. Another good tip: It helps to put a spot of glue on the tape measure under the bird, so it won't slip out.

We once filled a Christmas tree with birds in red and green prints. We used two florist's wires instead of the elastics, and eliminated the tape measure. We pushed the wires through the bird's body, approximately where the elastic is attached, then wrapped wires around the branches. These birds will sit better if you don't use the weighted pellets; use stuffing instead. For fun, make a birdcage from long willow branches. We tied a five-foot long bundle of them together at the top and bottom with raffia bows, and used a 12" grapevine wreath inside to make the willows spread into a round cage. We put a couple of twisted branches in the center for perches and wrapped ivy and flowering vines around some of the willows. Wire some birds inside on the wreath and on the perches, and then suspend the birdcage from the ceiling.

Supply List

Small print (1/8 yd. will make three birds)

Medium print (1/8 yd. will make two birds)

Small amount of stuffing

1/2 cup weighted pellets

Two 3mm round bead eyes or two black pins

Pin or end of a sharpened dowel for beak

Small scrap of heavy-weight interfacing

Optional:
Round tape measure, small embroidery scissors, seam ripper, 1/4 yd. of 1/4 " elastic

Cutting Instructions: Pattern pieces are on page 58. Cut two heads and two bodies from small print. Cut four wings, two of each tail, and two breasts from medium print. Cut one of each tail and two wings from medium to heavy-weight interfacing.

1. *Optional:* If you wish to attach sewing accessories, do this before starting: Topstitch across folded ends of a 1" long piece of elastic to the right side of the body, with ends tucked under 1/4" as shown. Repeat for other side, if desired. When bird is finished, you can slip scissors and seam ripper through under wings.

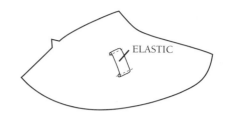

2a. Sew two wings, right sides together, to one layer of interfacing from A to B. Trim off tip of wing, trim seams, and clip to stitching. Turn right side out, press.

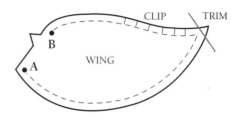

2b. Repeat for other wing, upper and lower tails.

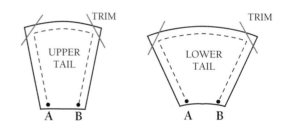

3. Place wing, right side up, on body, matching notches. Place head on top, match notch, ease, and sew head and wing to body.

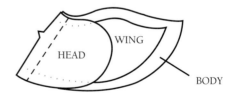

4. Sew two breasts, right sides together, from C to A, and B to D.

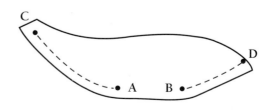

5. Pin heads together, matching neck seam. Sew from E on head to D at tip of tail.

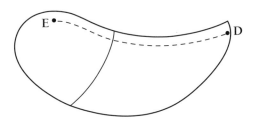

6. Center and pin two tails, lower tail on top, to seam at D.

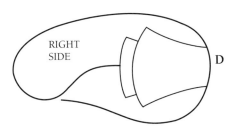

7. Pin breast on top of tails, right sides together, sew across tails, and up one side of breast to C. Backstitch 3 stitches.

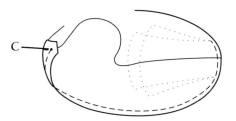

8. Then pin and sew from C, along opposite side of breast, to tail.

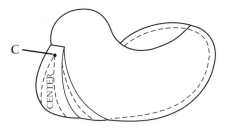

9. Finish sewing head from E to C, backstitch. Clip seam allowance free from stitching at tail and clip at back of neck and at C. Trim seam allowance to 1/8" over the top of the head.

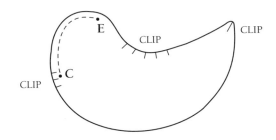

10. Turn right side out and stuff the tail a little, then the head firmly. Pour pellets into body, stuff them in firmly, then stitch opening closed. Sew on bead eyes or put pins in at an angle. Beak can be glued on, or put a pin in just 1/4" below eye on front seam. Sharpen the end of an 1/8" dowel, not quite to a point, cut off with wire cutters, for a wooden beak.

11a. Sew a button to the tip of the wing. Then, hand tack wing tip to body.

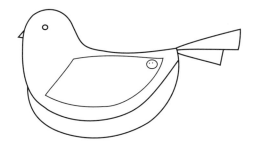

11b. Hand sew two elastic pieces 3" long in a loose X on bird underside, turn ends of elastic under 1/4". This elastic X holds a round, retractable tape measure.

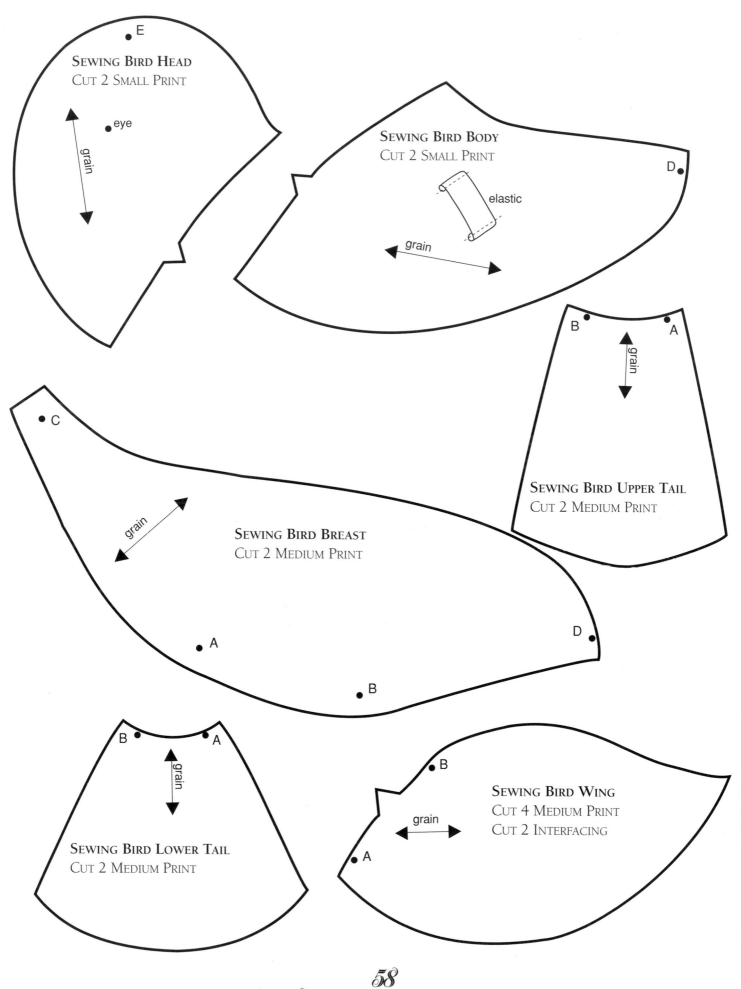

Sewing Bird Head
Cut 2 Small Print

E •

• eye

grain

Sewing Bird Body
Cut 2 Small Print

elastic

grain

D •

B • • A

grain

Sewing Bird Upper Tail
Cut 2 Medium Print

C •

grain

Sewing Bird Breast
Cut 2 Medium Print

• A

• B

D •

B • • A

grain

Sewing Bird Lower Tail
Cut 2 Medium Print

• B

grain

• A

Sewing Bird Wing
Cut 4 Medium Print
Cut 2 Interfacing

The house is old, the trees are bare
And moonless bends the misty dome,
But what on earth is half so dear,
So longed for, as the hearth of home.

—Emily Brontë

≈

Full many a glorious morning I have seen flatter

the mountain tops with sovereign eye, kissing with

golden face the meadows green, gilding pale streams with

heavenly alchemy;

—William Shakespeare
(Sonnet 33)

FATHER CHRISTMAS

©1991 Kathy Pace

For years I've loved the beautiful Santas available in doll shops, their porcelain faces with so much character carved into the wrinkles. I was discouraged even thinking about trying to create such splendor in cloth. Once I did do a couple of Santas on a smaller scale, more like simple rag dolls. I had it in my heart to do a really gorgeous embellished one, but the face just stopped me cold. I couldn't figure out how to do it.

Then, one day, Dennis and I were visiting quilt shops and antiquing through Nebraska. We stopped at one store where they offered a Santa-of-the-Month class. The Santas were unbelievable. They were as varied as they could be, but all detailed and wonderful. I wondered if there was a Santa that hadn't been done yet, or how I could dream of going beyond all that had been done. It was inspiring and discouraging all at once. As we drove on toward home, I thought about some beautifully crafted crazy quilts we had seen on our travels. The colors were dark and rich, with old hair ribbons, promotional pendant ties, pieces of ball gowns and velvet cloaks. The fancy stitches were worked in perle cotton and silk threads. I began to think about the Santa I'd love to do if I could get the head right and, while Dennis drove the long stretches of highway, I drew a Santa on a scrap of paper. I thought of a cape that would be pointed in back with a tassel at the bottom. How different it would be if it were all crazy-quilted and embellished with little stars, hearts, buttons, beads, flowers, and everything else I could find. As soon as we got home, I started working on my own Father Christmas. His face wasn't as hard as I thought it would be! Just a big nose and a few stitches to accentuate it, then cover his face with a beard, and voilà! We used a little gray braided hair mixed in with the white for an older look; even the unwashed curly lamb's wool with its original kinks and twists works well. The fun part is the embellishing, so the body is just a simple rag-doll style that gives a foundation to his marvelous clothes.

There's lots of room for imagination here. I'm still having fun with this Santa. Each one we make is different, and I can't wait to see the next one! It is like having Christmas each time a new Father Christmas is completed. I helped my mother make a great Santa from interesting old fabrics and trimmings. She embellished him by tying a twine loop over one shoulder and hanging it almost to his coat hem. (I've since used braid, cord, or fancy ribbon in place of the twine.) Then she tied knots 1" to 2" apart along the cord and to those tied little toys and ornaments — wagon, sled, doll, horn, drum, baskets of lace, saw, clock-face button, tree, cuckoo clock, picture frame. He is loaded, and he looks marvelous. She trimmed his red wool jacquard coat with brown rabbit fur. His boots complete the picture with buckles from a woman's gloves. For his mittens, we carefully cut up a pair of woman's gloves and placed the tucks on the original gloves on the backs of his hands.

Antique shops and second-hand stores have lots of little treasures to make a one-of-a-kind Santa. During my trips I've picked up an old green spice box just the right size to be a present, a small tin sheep, a green feather for his hat or shoulder, old black braid and a snippet of black beaded lace, a navy blue beaded bodice from an old flapper dress and a shoe buckle with metal beads just right for his belt, a length of black beaded twist cord, a tiny teapot, a little round red watch case, a tiny toy iron, and two little old glass bottles. Hang lots of tiny objects from his arms and elbows at different lengths: wreaths, candy canes, cradles, trains, a tricycle. Try fancy frogs and big fancy buttons to close his coat — although I usually leave it open to show off his pants, shoes, and belt buckle. I wondered about putting wire in the hem of his coat to hold its shape or even hold it blown-open-seeming in front, but that wasn't necessary because corduroy is stiff enough to stand out on its own. I'd like to see him wear a charm necklace or bracelet with stars, hearts, and other toys attached. On one Father Christmas we put a fancy beaded bracelet over his hat from ear to ear, just for something different from pine cones and berries.

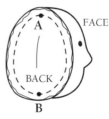

Supply List

1/2 yd. tan fabric with matching thread
20 1/2" of woolly crepe doll hair, white
(Ours is dyed in a cup of Lipton Tea,
then dried thoroughly before separating.)
Two 9mm round black craft eyes
Doll stand for a 24" doll
1/2 yd. muslin or any lightweight cotton fabric
Scraps of corduroy, velvet, satin, and other
similar fabrics in prints, solids, stripes, etc.,
in coordinating colors (black, tan, green,
navy, rose print, paisley, stripes, cranberry)
for crazy quilted cape.
Perle cotton or embroidery floss in
coordinating colors.
Beads, buttons, charms, old jewelry, a large
brooch, etc. for embellishments
1/2 yd. cotton in coordinating color for cape lining
1 1/4 yds. of 3/8" rope twist
30 oz. stuffing
One 3" black tassel
1 1/3 yds. of 2" black satin ribbon
1/2 yd. of 1/2"-wide fur for trim
1 yd. coat fabric — corduroy, wool, velvet, etc.
Small tassel, berries, small pine cones
Florist's wire and brown florist's tape
to curl on hat
1/3 yd. gold twist cord for hat
1/2 yd. of 1"-wide green wired ribbon for hat
1/8 yd. felt or Ultrasuede® or Facile® for boots and
mittens or 1/8 yd. of each color
1/2 yd. fabric for pants
One 3/8" button for pants
Two black frogs (optional, to close coat)
Three small 2" birds, various small toys
2 yds. tasseled braid trim
28" brushed nylon for bag
2 3/4 yds. braid trim
1 yd. twist cord and ribbon for bag bow
Disappearing marking pen
Tacky glue or glue gun

When you assemble fabrics for the crazy-quilted cape, remember you'll need a lot of solid fabrics or neutrals to go between your prints. When I make a red and green (or a purple and green one), the neutrals I use are tan, navy, brown, and a lot of black. One of my favorite Santas had black pants and a deep purple corduroy coat. His cape was purples and greens with neutrals, plus light lavender and light green. He was beautiful! Let your imagination wander freely with this doll.

Father Christmas' Body

Cutting Instructions: All pattern pieces will be found on the pull-out pages at the back of this book. Cut two right arms, two left arms, one seat, four legs (with trimmed tops of two inside legs as indicated on pattern). Cut two faces, one head back from tan fabric.

1a. Sew two faces together, A to B. Clip curves.

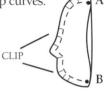

1b. Gather outside edge of back of head, and sew to faces, right sides together, matching dots A and B. Put safety eyes in. Stuff firmly. Whipstitch opening closed.

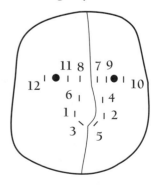

2. Trace stitch positions onto right and left faces, using a disappearing marker. Secure a strong matching thread at the back of the head, come out at stitch 1. Take a small (1/8" long) stitch, go through the nose, and stuffing 1/4" deep, and come out at stitch 2. Take a small stitch and come out at stitch 1 again. Pull the stitches gently until desired pucker appears. Go out back of head and secure thread with a backstitch, and knot while holding puckers in place. Proceed the same way for stitches 3 and 4, 5 and 6, 7 and 8. Come out at 9 and go into back of head, pull and tie off. Repeat for stitches 10, 11 and 12, to flatten eye area.

3. Sew two right arms together from A to B and C to D. Clip curves turn right side out. Repeat for left arm pieces.

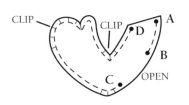

CLIP

CLIP

D

A

B

C

OPEN

4a. Lay out two legs opposite each other. Sew one inside leg to one outside leg from A to B. Clip inside curve. Turn right side out and stuff firmly to within 1" of opening.

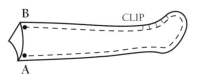

B

CLIP

A

4b. Sew across top with seams matching. Repeat for other leg.

SEAMS

5a. Matching notches, sew legs and seat to body front, toes down. (Place seat over legs.)

SEAT

5b. Fold legs down and pin arms in place with raw edges even. Pin second body over arms and sew as shown up one side, across top, and down other side.

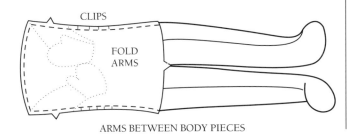

CLIPS

FOLD ARMS

ARMS BETWEEN BODY PIECES

6. Turn body right side out, stuff arms and body. Whipstitch seat to lower edge of back body. Close off arm openings. Whipstitch head to center of top of body.

7. Cut fake hair braid into the following lengths: two 3/4" for eye brows; two 2" for hair; three 4" for beard; one 3" for mustache. For all but mustache, separate lengths gently, but not completely, leaving some kinks and clumps. For mustache, don't separate center; separate ends only. Glue in place with tacky glue. Eyebrows are very close to the eye, almost covering the top of the eye.

7a. Glue beard upside down to a point even with the eye at the seam line.

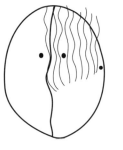

7b. Then fold it down and stick it firmly onto the face.

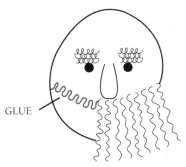

GLUE

7c. Place a line of glue around the back of head straight across from top corners of the beard. Stick hair onto it.

7d. After Santa is dressed, carefully blend separated beard strands with non-separated ones, and trim beard in a U shape.

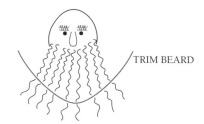

TRIM BEARD

Father Christmas' Crazy-Quilted Cape

Note: The inspiration and how-tos for this cape came from Judith Montano and her book Crazy Quilt Odyssey.

Cutting Instructions: All pattern pieces will be found on the pull-out pages at the back of this book. Cut one cape back and two fronts from muslin and cut the same pieces from coordinating-colored cotton for lining. Cut one crazy quilt beginning piece from a printed fabric.

1a. Place beginning piece on cape back slightly off center. Cut 2"-wide rectangles or strips from prints, solids or subtly textured fabrics for crazy quilting.

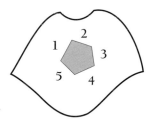

1b. Start by sewing one rectangular piece to the edge of the beginning piece, right sides together.

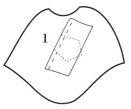

1c. Then turn rectangle over, right side up, and press.

STRIP 1

CENTER

2. Sew a second wide rectangle to angle 2. (Lefthanded people may want to go counterclockwise.) Trim off excess seam allowance, turn rectangle to right side, and press.

SEW

3. Sew a rectangle to third angle, trim away underneath, and press to right side. Sew rectangles to fourth and fifth angles as before. Be sure to cover angle and complete width of previous piece.

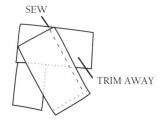

SEW

TRIM AWAY

4a. Then cut angles in rectangular pieces to make at least six or more angles again. Trim on dotted lines. Work around new angles adding rectangular pieces as before. Rectangular pieces tend to get longer.

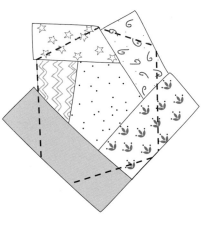

4b. If your piece is too long to look nice, piece a rectangular strip from pie-shaped wedges, cut a straight edge from one side and use it in place of one solid rectangle. When cape piece is covered, trim piecing to match raw edges of cape. Zigzag around outside edge to hold piecing to cape. *Note: You may want to add braids or ribbons to each piece as it is machine sewn in place. However, I like to add them on top of the finished crazy quilt work, and turn the raw ends under, or snip a few stitches and tuck it inside a seam. Then hide the entry with a button or bead cluster.

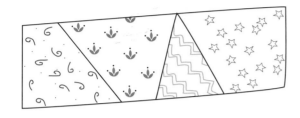

5. Add a beaded appliqué, old lace, or trims. Machine stitch with decorative stitches over seams; handsew seed beads, glass pebble beads, tassels, metal charms, old jewelry, lockets and other embellishments at random. Stay 1/2" away from outside edges of all seams. Cover the two crazy-quilted front pieces of cape by the same method. Remember that the beard will cover most of the center front.

5a. Sew cape together on shoulder seams, right sides together. Repeat for lining.

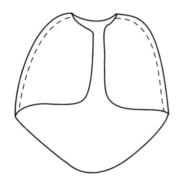

5b. Then sew lining to cape with neck open. Clip curves, turn right side out through neck, and gently press from lining side.

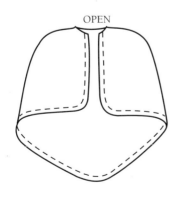

OPEN

5c. Hand-sew wide cord to edge of cape. Add tassel. Tape over ends of cord to keep them from unraveling.

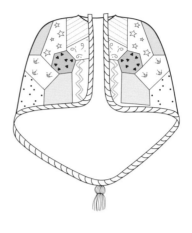

Father Christmas' Coat and Hat Patterns

Cutting Instructions: All pattern pieces will be found on the pull-out pages at the back of this book. Cut from fabric: two sleeves, one back yoke, one back facing, one back, four fronts, (two fronts are facings), and two hats. Cut from fur: two sleeve trims, two coat front trims, one coat back trim, one hat trim.

1. Finish raw edge of facings by zigzaging near edge. Set aside.

BACK

FRONT

2. Sew two hats together from A to B. Clip curves and turn right side out. Set aside.

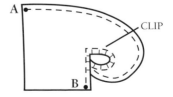

A · · · CLIP

B

3a. Gather top of coat back. Sew right sides together to back yoke. Sew fur trim to lower edge of coat, with fur side up (right side of fur to wrong side of coat back) underneath coat back. (Right side of coat up.)

RIGHT SIDE UP

EDGES
ARE EVEN

3b. Turn fur to right side of coat. Turn under 1/4" of top edge of fur and hand whipstitch fur to the coat.

3c. Repeat fur trim process on sleeves and front edge of hat. Topstitch tassel-braid trim along edge of fur on sleeve. Turn up lower edge of the hat to wrong side 1/4" twice and topstitch. Put small amount of stuffing in curly end of hat.

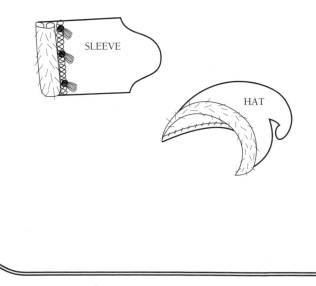

SLEEVE

HAT

3d. Add beads, charms, and a small tassel to curly end of hat. Sew gold twist cord, berries, and pine cones in bunches to the top of the hat. You may want to cover the florist's wire with brown florist's tape and curl it around a pencil. Tack 1/2" sections to the hat between bunches of pine cones and berries. Cut green wire ribbon in half. Make two 1 1/2" loops in one end of ribbon. Sew loops to the hat at lower front corner. Repeat for other half of ribbon, attaching to other corner. Leave untied. Sew hat to head at lower corners. Cover all of his forehead.

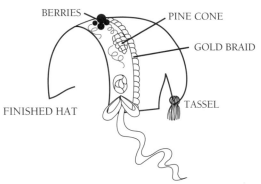

BERRIES

PINE CONE

GOLD BRAID

FINISHED HAT

TASSEL

4. Sew fur trim to coat fronts on trim line, right sides together and using a 1/4" seam allowance on fur. Turn fur right side up and pin to edge of coat front, matching raw edges.

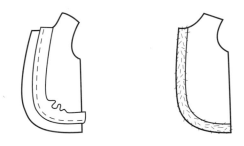

5a. Sew coat front to back at shoulder seam, right sides together.

5b. Gather top of sleeve. Open coat out flat, sew sleeve in armhole, right sides together. Repeat for the other sleeve.

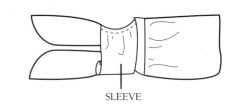

SLEEVE

6a. Sew front facings to back facing at shoulders.

6b. Sew facings to coat, right sides together, from A to B. Clip curves, turn facing to inside, and press.

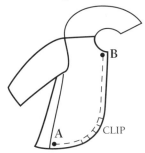

6c. Sew underarm seam with sleeve and coats right sides together. Matching hems, and underarm seams. Keep facing out of the way. (See Step 7 below.)

7. Pin cape to coat matching raw edges at the neck, with coat and cape right side out (wrong side of cape to right side of coat). Cape just meets fur trim. Turn facing wrong side out on top of cape (right side of facing to right side of cape). Sew around neck from B to B. Clip to stitching, turn facing to inside, and tack it down at the shoulder seam.

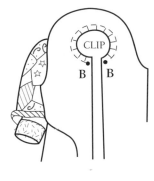

8a. Fold side seam edge of facing under 1/4" and whip-stitch over seam allowances of coat's side seam.

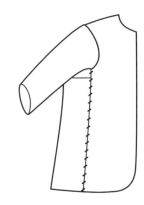

8b. On right side, topstitch tassel braid trim near fur on fronts and back with ends hidden under cape fronts. Tack frogs to coat front.

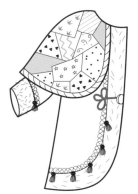

9a. Leaving 1 1/2" tails at both ends, machine sew down center of black ribbon while tucking ribbon into 1/4" folds toward needle and then away from the needle as you sew.

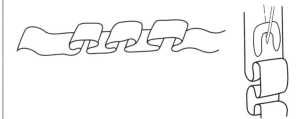

9b. Fold ribbon in half right side out along stitching line. Sew to cape 1/8" from neck edge.

Father Christmas' Boots, Mittens, and Pants

Cutting Instructions: All pattern pieces will be found on the pull-out pages at the back of this book. Cut four boots and four mittens from Ultrasuede®.

1. Sew two mittens from A to B, clip curves, and turn right side out. Glue around open edge of mitten onto hand.

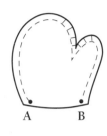

2a. Sew two boots from A to B, clip to dots, clip curves, and turn right side out.

2b. Sew from A to C and B to D. Turn top of boot down.

2c. Sew cross stitch laces in place, with perle cotton or floss. Sew beads at ends of each X.

3a. Cut two pants as indicated. Cut one waistband. Sew one side seam with pants right sides together and then gather the top edge of the pants. Sew waistband to pants right sides together. Leave 1" of waistband on one side, 1/4" on the other side. Zigzag-hem edges of pants.

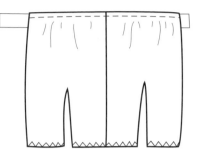

3b. Fold waist band as shown. Sew across ends. Turn right side out. Hand whipstitch to inside of pants.

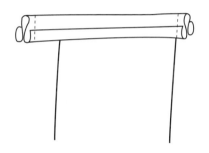

3c. Make a buttonhole in one end of band. Sew button to other end.

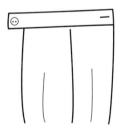

4a. Fold pants in half right sides together, and sew as shown.

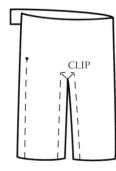

4b. Turn right side out and place on Santa. Glue to ankles with little tucks. Pull boots on. Put coat on and tack coat fronts together under beard. Glue birds to hand and shoulder. Use twist cord and pretty ribbons to hang toys from his arms. Dust his cheeks and nose with powder blush if desired.

Father Christmas' Bag

1. Make a 28" fabric square. Fold in fourths so all edges are even. Fold again in a pie shape. Make a mark at 14" on fold and cut, rounding corner off. Open out circle and sew braid trim to right side just covering raw edge of the fabric. Fold braid to wrong side and topstitch. Put stuffing in, and tie bag loosely with twist cord and ribbon. Glue toys and books in top of the bag.

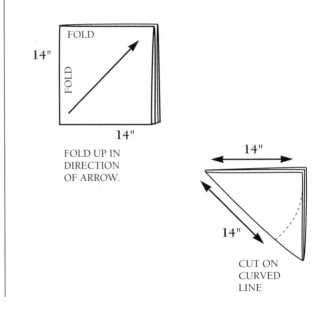

OUR OLD-FASHIONED ELF

©1992 Kathy Pace

Do you remember the Little Golden Book with the story of Santa's workshop? I haven't seen it for many years, but I can recall pages where little elves were making and painting toys. One was painting a red smile on a pretty doll. Some were hammering on trains or trucks. There is in my memory an impression of how the elves were dressed. When I designed the elf pattern, I tried to be true to how I remembered the elves in that book. Their clothes weren't fancy or Victorian: they wore simple brown jerkins, soft pointed shoes, and shirts with puffy sleeves. I love details, like their real leather belts with a few keys hanging from a cord. These things lend a feeling of reality to our elf pattern. It brings back the excitement of childhood, when we believed that toys could come to life while we were sleeping or unaware. When a child looks at the elf's keys, she wonders what elf-sized treasure box or cottage door they will open. That is the magic of childhood I hope our elf brings back to us. Little things can spark our imagination and take us on the same flights of fancy still, if we allow ourselves the moment it takes to notice and enjoy them. On the original drawings of the elf, I included an overall-style work apron with pockets and a tiny leather lunch pouch strung over one shoulder and across his chest. Each elf you make will have his own identity and secrets to share; how you decorate him will help complete your own fantasy.

Medium to large prints can be used on the elf's hat with pleasing results; medium to small prints look best for his jerkin and pants. Thin velour that looks like crushed velvet comes in such beautiful colors, and it makes wonderful elf clothes. Deep green and teal hats and purple or burgundy jerkins give the elf a very rich and elegant appearance. Try to find a stripe for his legs that is less than 1/2" wide: narrow stripes look better than wide because he is not very tall. Some of the old leather belts we've used were as wide as 2", with double prongs on the buckle. The ones that look the best are about 3/4" wide

SUPPLY LIST

1/3 yd. tan fabric for body

1/3 yd. stripe fabric for legs

Two 8mm black safety eyes

6" braided doll hair

Matching threads
(heavy tan craft thread is helpful also)

Stuffing

Tacky or hot glue

One old thin leather belt

3/8 yd. fabric for hat with matching thread

One small tassel, approximately 3"
(or 3/4" bell and assorted buttons)

3/8 yd. piping (optional)

3/4 yd. of 1/4" satin cord for mittens

1/4 yd. fabric for mittens and boots

7/8 yd. of 1/8" satin cord for boots

1/3 yd. tan or brown fabric for pants

1 yd. of 1/4" elastic

1/2 yd. light print or muslin for shirt

Three 3/8" buttons and matching thread

2/3 yd. ribbon for neck

3/8 yd. fabric for jerkin

One tan 3/8" button for jerkin

Disappearing marking pen

71

THE BEST FROM GOOSEBERRY HILL

and in a color that matches the rest of his clothes. Tie little tools to his belt, or a pocket watch. A cluster of star, heart, and moon charms could be tied onto his key ring.

If you need a St. Patrick's Day decoration, just dress him in green for a leprechaun. Put a bunch of shamrocks in his fist and use red braided hair in place of the white. Try gluing his legs on with his feet up on the table, so his knees are in the air. Put a small clay flowerpot or a basket between his knees, and fill it with gold foil chocolate coins.

Elf's Body

Note: It is possible, but not recommended to use moveable doll joints on this project. The legs would attach at dot H, the arms at I, the head at F on body, to the corresponding notches on the body. See joint package for detailed instructions. Use 2 1/2" joints for arms and legs, 1 1/2" joint for head.

Cutting Instructions: Pattern pieces will be found on the pull-out pages at the back of this book. Cut two faces (mark eyes and sculpting stitches with disappearing pen), two head backs, four ears, two body fronts, two body backs, four arms from tan fabric. Cut four legs from stripe fabric, matching stripes for each pair.

1a. Sew two head backs together from A to B and C to D.

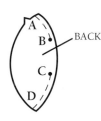

1b. Sew two faces from A to D as shown. Clip curves.

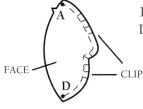

1c. Sew faces to head backs, matching dots A and D as shown. Put in safety eyes. Turn right side out, stuff, and whipstitch opening closed.

1d. Sculpt lip as follows. With a doll needle, and a doubled thread, secure a knot in the back of the head with a couple of back stitches. Come out 1/2" below the bottom of the nose, take a 1/4" stitch, go 1/4" deep and come out just below the nose. Make another 1/4" stitch, go 1/4" deep, and come out again at first stitch. Pull firmly to make a nice lip. Go into the head and out the back. Secure thread with a knot.

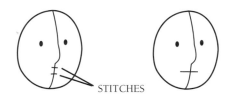

STITCHES

2a. To sculpt nose, go in the back of the head, come out 1/2" to the side of the nose, about 3/4" above lower edge of nose. Make a stitch, go through face, not too deep (1/4" or so), and come out even with lower edge of nose. Make a stitch, coming out at first stitch and pulling gently to make side of nose. Go out back of the head, and secure. Repeat for other side of nose.

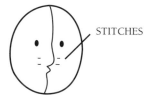

STITCHES

2b. Then repeat this process for stitches 5 and 6, 7 and 8, 9 and 10. Take stitches straight through from the back of the head to the front for stitches 11, 12, 13, and 14. These pull the eyes a little flatter.

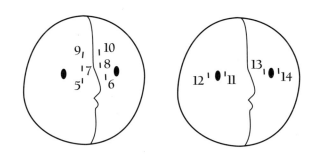

2c. Sew two ears as shown, turn right side out through the slit on one ear. Stuff slightly. Top stitch as shown. Glue in place to the face as indicated with top of ear free. Repeat for other ear.

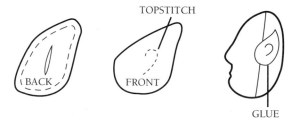

2d. Separate two 2" strands of braided doll hair and glue to back of head so hair begins even with middle of ears and ends even with bottom edge of head. Cut and separate 1" braid into three pieces. Glue one little bunch just over each eye and under nose. Cut and separate another 1" strand into two pieces. Glue in front of each ear. Hat covers the rest of the head, and tops of hair.

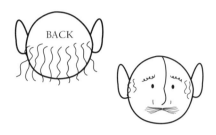

3a. Sew two body fronts together on un-notched edges. Sew two body backs together from A to B and C to D. Place fronts on backs, right sides together, matching notches and seams. Sew all around outside edge. Mark notch locations on right side with pencil dots, for top of body, arms and legs. Turn right side out, stuff, close off opening.

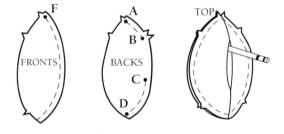

3b. Sew two arms together from A to B. Clip curves, turn right side out, stuff, then whipstitch opening closed. Stuff hand only slightly, so you can bend it later if desired. Repeat for other arm. After you have dressed the elf, use stitches and glue to hold items in his hands.

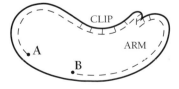

4a. Sew two legs right sides together from A to B. Clip curves, trim off point, turn right side out, stuff foot softly, and legs more firmly. Whipstitch opening closed. Repeat for other leg.

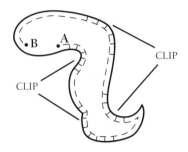

4b. Sew or glue head to top of body, match seams of head and body where they cross. Legs should be centered so dot H matches leg notch on body so body sits nicely on edge of table. Match dot I on arms to body notches, with one hand higher than the other if desired. Legs and body should touch the table. He should sit easily without tipping. Legs can also be attached so the elf sits on a table.

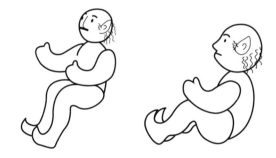

Elf's Pants

Cutting Instructions: Pattern will be found on the pull-out pages at the back of this book. Cut two pants on fold.

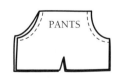

1a. Open pants out flat. With right sides together sew two crotch curves.

1b. Refold on fold lines and sew inner leg seam.

1c. Hem pant legs by turning them up 1/4" to wrong side twice and sewing.

1d. Sew from A to B on both pant legs. On outside sew two little buttons near dots B. Then turn down top edge of pants 1/8" then 1/2" to wrong side to form casing for elastic. Leave opening at back to thread 15" of elastic through. Sew across ends of elastic.

Elf's Shirt

Cutting Instructions: Pattern pieces will be found on pages 78-79 and on the pull-out pages at the back of this book. Cut two sleeves, one shirt back, two fronts, two back facings, two front facings, two front yokes from muslin or light print.

1a. Gather top of sleeves. Make casing at sleeve hem by turning hem up 1/4" then 3/8" and sew. Thread 5" of elastic through casings and stitch across ends.

1b. Gather top edges of shirt fronts and shirt back between stars.

1c. With right sides together, sew notched edge of front yoke to shirt front matching notches. Repeat for other front. Sew one back facing as a back yoke to shirt back.

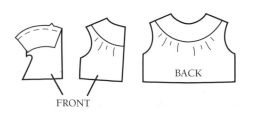

2a. Sew shoulder seams of remaining back facing to front facings. Serge or zigzag outer edge.

2b. Sew shirt fronts to backs at shoulder seams, right sides together. Open out flat.

2c. Sew sleeves to armholes right sides together. Sew facings to shirt, right sides together. Stitch across lower edge and up around neck. Clip to stitching around neck and press to inside.

2d. Sew underarm seams, with shirt right sides together. Hem lower edge to wrong side, with a narrow hemming foot, or simply turn up 1/4" and sew. Make buttonholes as indicated in left side, and sew buttons on underneath. Place shirt on elf and tie ribbon bow around his neck.

Elf's Jerkin

Cutting Instructions: Pattern pieces will be found on the pull-out pages at the back of this book. Cut two peplums, two backs, and four fronts.

1a. Sew shoulder seams of two fronts to one back, repeat for remaining pieces (lining).

1b. Place lining, right sides together on top of front and

back. Sew as shown. Clip curves. Turn right side out through back and press.

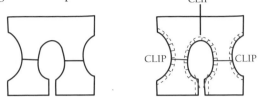

1c. Open sides and sew fronts to backs at side seams right sides together.

2a. Sew two peplums, right sides together at one short edge. Make a narrow hem on front edges and lower edge by turning under to wrong side 1/4" twice. Gather top edge to fit lower edge of jerkin.

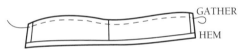

2b. Sew peplum to one layer only on lower edge of right side of jerkin.

2c. Turn up remaining edge of jerkin lining 1/4" to wrong side, pin, then whip in place.

2d. Make a buttonhole in left front and sew button in place on right side.

Elf's Belt

1. Belt: to keep the old belt holes, measure 8" from the buckle and cut off the belt. Then buckle the belt as you want it, and wrap the long end over the cut end overlapping 1/2". Mark and cut long end of belt. Machine sew or hot glue the overlap.

Elf's Hat

Cutting Instructions: Pattern will be found on the pull-out pages at the back of this book. Cut one hat.

1a. Sew piping to right side of lower edge, 3/8" from edge as shown.

1b. Fold hat right sides together. Sew from A to B. Turn right side out.

1c. Turn up lower edge 3/8" to wrong side and topstitch 1/4" from piping. Then hand sew from dot A to dot C with long stitches inside the hat and short ones outside. Stuff a little stuffing in the hat above dot C. Pull up hand stitches to desired look. Backstitch and tie off inside hat. Sew a tassel, (we cut the fringe off a 3" tassel) to dot A. Stuff hat more if needed. Glue to head and hair just above eyebrows in front, and pull it down in back to cover the back of the head.

Elf's Boots

Cutting Instructions: Pattern will be found on the pull-out pages at the back of this book. Cut four boots and four boot linings (could be a contrasting color).

1a. Sew one boot lining to one boot right sides together from A to B. Clip to stitching at A and B. Turn right side out press. Repeat for opposite side of boot.

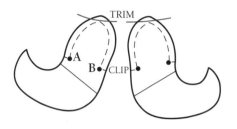

1b. Place two boots right sides together and sew from A to B around foot of boot. Trim off point and clip to stitching at curves. Turn right side out. Work onto foot and tie a 1/8" cord around ankle. Repeat for other boot.

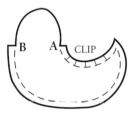

Elf's Mittens

Cutting Instructions: Pattern will be found on the pull-out pages at the back of this book. Cut two mitten fronts and two backs.

2a. Fold one back on one fold line wrong sides together and stitch a needle's width from fold. Repeat for other two fold lines. Backstitch to begin and end.

2b. Pin mitten front and back right sides together. Sew around mitten from A to B, clip curves, and turn right side out. Turn under cuff 1/4" to wrong side and sew near fold. Repeat for other mitten. Make knots in ends of 1/4" satin cord. Sew knots to back edge of each mitten.

Christmas Sewing Joys

While children sleep and dream sweet dreams,

Mother sews doll quilts with neat little seams.

She made a bear from Father's fur coat,

With shoe-button eyes, red tie 'round his throat.

Now an angel she fashions with Grandma's old lace;

She smiles as she stitches the sweet little face.

While her children may love these beautiful toys,

Sewing them brings her such secret joys!

≈

—Kathy Pace
Christmas 1992

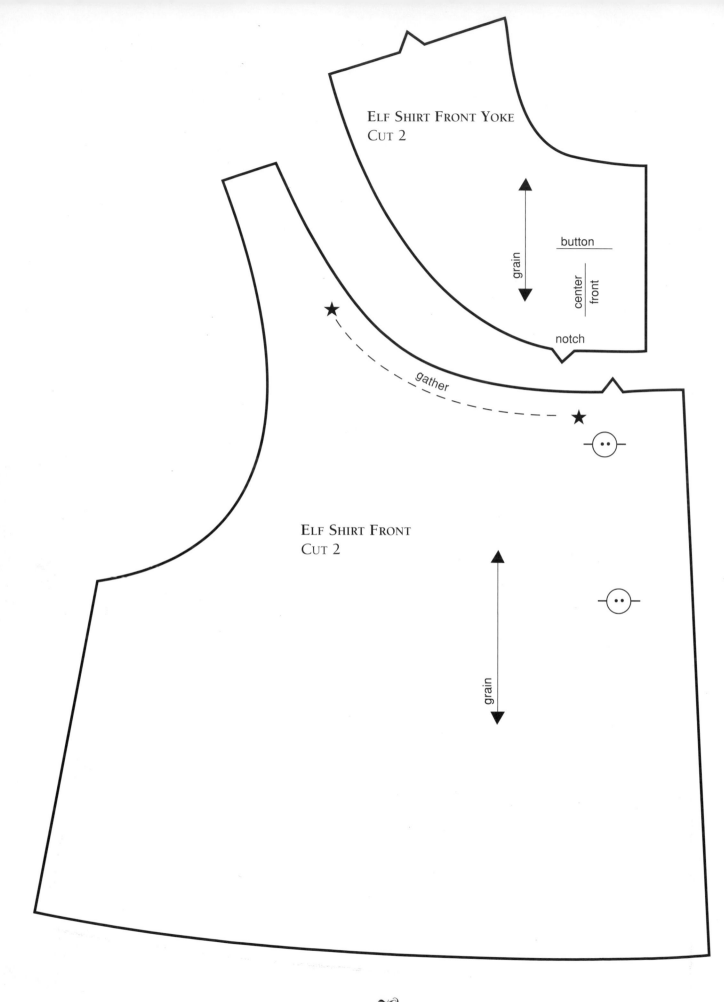

ELF SHIRT FRONT YOKE
CUT 2

grain

button

center front

notch

gather

ELF SHIRT FRONT
CUT 2

grain

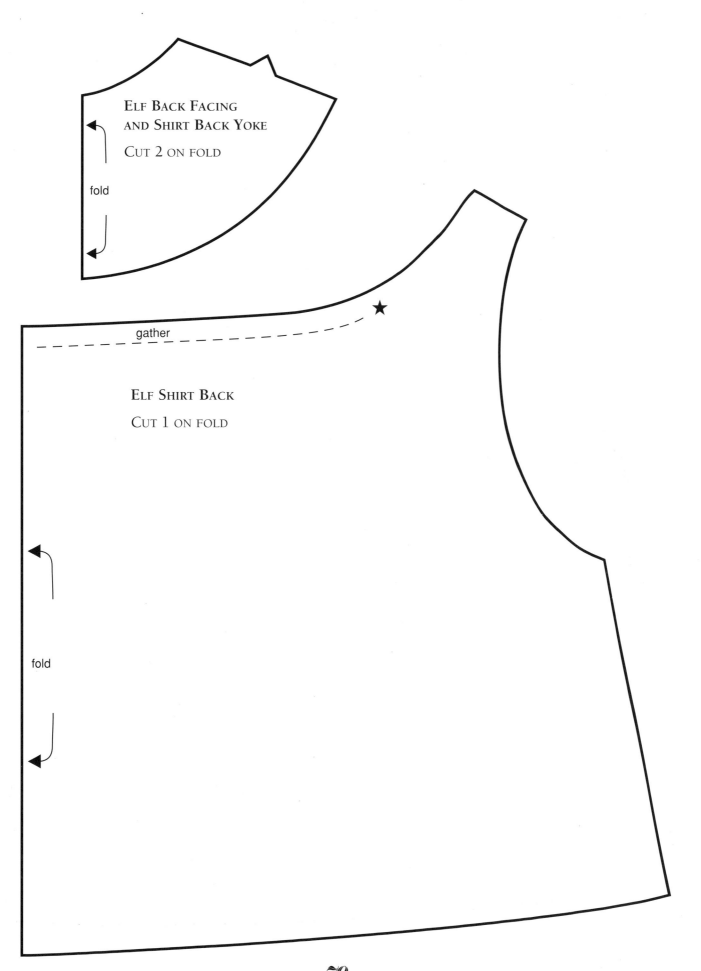

ELF BACK FACING
AND SHIRT BACK YOKE

CUT 2 ON FOLD

fold

gather

ELF SHIRT BACK

CUT 1 ON FOLD

fold

ABOUT THE AUTHOR

Kathy Pace is the owner and primary designer for Gooseberry Hill Pattern Company where she has done all of the designing, photography set-up, and instructional work for the company's 90-plus patterns.

Kathy was raised in Richland, Washington, and attended Brigham Young University in Provo, Utah, where she met Dennis Pace. She now lives near Coalville, Utah, in a high mountain valley. She loves the outdoors, and chose to raise her five children where they could hike and explore the beauties of unspoiled nature. Kathy is active in church service, the PTA, and several clubs. She loves to sew and collect antiques, especially old bears, dolls, buttons, and lace. Kathy also enjoys traveling, reading, entertaining, and decorating the family's log home for the holidays.

Kathy wrote and published a quarterly newsletter for Gooseberry Hill guild members for two years. She received a local Business Woman of the Year award in 1990. Her company has received some of the best booth awards at international quilt markets. She has been designing clothing and toys for McCall's Pattern Company of New York since 1991.

Kathy has taught many sewing and crafts classes in a variety of subjects from dried flower arranging to fancy embroidery. She has also taught classes on making bears at conferences, universities, and at the International Quilt Market in Houston. Gooseberry Hill has produced an instructional video in which Kathy demonstrates how to make one of the company's jointed bears out of mohair fur, and gives dressing as well as decorating tips.

Kathy's most cherished treasures are her husband, children, and friends.

OTHER FINE QUILTING BOOKS

FROM C & T PUBLISHING

Appliqué 12 Easy Ways!, Elly Sienkiewicz
The Art of Silk Ribbon Embroidery, Judith Montano
Baltimore Album Quilts, Historic Notes and Antique Patterns,
  Elly Sienkiewicz
Baltimore Beauties and Beyond (2 Volumes), Elly Sienkiewicz
A Celebration of Hearts, Jean Wells and Marina Anderson
Christmas Traditions From the Heart, Margaret Peters
Crazy Quilt Handbook, Judith Montano
Crazy Quilt Odyssey, Judith Montano
Design a Baltimore Album Quilt!, Elly Sienkiewicz
Dimensional Appliqué, Elly Sienkiewicz
Friendship's Offering, Susan McKelvey
Heirloom Machine Quilting, Harriet Hargrave
Imagery on Fabric, Jean Ray Laury
Isometric Perspective, Katie Pasquini-Masopust
The Magical Effects of Color, Joen Wolfrom
Mastering Machine Appliqué, Harriet Hargrave

Memorabilia Quilting, Jean Wells
NSA Series: Bloomin' Creation; Holiday Happenings;
  Hometown; Hearts, Fans, Folk Art, Jean Wells
Pattern Play, Doreen Speckmann
PQME Series: Milky Way Quilt; Nine-Patch Quilt; Pinwheel
  Quilt; Stars & Hearts Quilt, Jean Wells
Quilts, Quilts, and More Quilts!, Diana McClun & Laura Nownes
Recollections, Judith Montano
Stitching Free: Easy Machine Pictures, Shirley Nilsson
A Treasury of Quilt Labels, Susan McKelvey
Visions: The Art of the Quilt, Quilt San Diego
Whimsical Animals, Miriam Gourley

For more information write for a free catalog from
C & T Publishing
P.O. Box 1456
Lafayette, CA 94549